THE GULF WAR OF 1991 RECONSIDERED

The **Begin–Sadat (BESA) Center for Strategic Studies at Bar-Ilan University** is dedicated to the study of Middle East peace and security, in particular the national security and foreign policy of Israel. A non-partisan and independent institute, the BESA Center is named in memory of Menachem Begin and Anwar Sadat, whose efforts in pursuing peace laid the cornerstone for future conflict resolution in the Middle East.

Since its founding in 1991 by Dr Thomas O. Hecht of Montreal, the BESA Center has become one of the most dynamic Israeli research institutions. It has developed cooperative relationships with strategic study centers throughout the world, from Ankara to Washington and from London to Seoul. Among its research staff are some of Israel's best and brightest academic and military minds. BESA Center publications and policy recommendations are read by senior Israeli decision-makers, in military and civilian life, by academicians, the press and the broader public.

The BESA Center makes its research available to the international community through three publication series: BESA *Security and Policy Studies*, BESA *Colloquia on Strategy and Diplomacy* and BESA *Studies in International Security*. The Center also sponsors conferences, symposia, workshops, lectures and briefings for international and local audiences.

Contents

Part IV: The United States

Part V: A Retrospective

Notes on Contributors

Andrew J. Bacevich is Professor of International Relations at Boston University and Director of the Center for International Relations. Prior to his academic career, he served for 23 years as an officer in the United States Army.

Gabriel Ben-Dor is Professor of Political Science at the University of Haifa and heads the Center for National Security Studies. He also serves as advisor to the Knesset Committee on Defense and Foreign Affairs.

Stuart A. Cohen is Professor of Political Studies at Bar-Ilan University and a senior research associate at the BESA Center for Strategic Studies.

F. Gregory Gause, III is Associate Professor of Political Science at the University of Vermont, and Director of the University's Middle East Studies Program.

Efraim Inbar is professor of Political Studies at Bar-Ilan University and director of the BESA Center for Strategic Studies.

Efraim Karsh is Professor and Head of Mediterranean Studies at King's College, University of London.

Michael T. Klare is the Five College Professor of Peace and World Security Studies based at Hampshire College, Amherst, Massachusetts and Director of the Five College Program in Peace and World Security Studies (PAWSS).

Thomas G. Mahnken is Professor of Strategy and Policy at the US Naval War College, Newport, Rhode Island. He participated in the Gulf War Air Power Survey and served in the US Defense Department's Office of Net Assessment.

Preface

The Iraqi conquest of Kuwait in August 1990 and the ensuing Gulf War of 1991 marked something of a watershed in the international history of the Middle East. The Iraqi attempt to eliminate a sister-state was unusual in inter-Arab relations, even considering the precarious legitimacy of the Middle Eastern borders, drawn by the former colonial powers. Although Arab states have by no means treated Arab borders as sacrosanct – as Syria's transformation of Lebanon into a virtual protectorate and North Yemen's absorption of South Yemen attest – Kuwait's elimination as an independent state was something quite different. The combination of Saddam Hussein's large ambitions, Iraq's military potential and the prospect of further Iraqi aggression meant that the assault on this very small (albeit very rich) country constituted a significant threat for Iraq's immediate and more distant neighbors. This accounts for the unprecedented willingness of major regional actors, Saudi Arabia in particular, to see the United States intervene at the head of an international military coalition to restore the *status quo ante*.

When the mere threat of military force proved insufficient to dislodge Iraqi troops from Kuwait, the US-led coalition in January 1991 launched Operation Desert Storm. Saddam Hussein had once again miscalculated and Iraq found itself on the losing end of a second Gulf War. The coalition's spectacular military victory restored the rule of the Sabah family in Kuwait and reenergized the Arab–Israeli peace process. At the Madrid peace conference, convening in October 1991, the overwhelming majority of the Arab states sat for the first time ever at the negotiating table with Israel. With the demonstration of American military might having raised respect for (and perhaps fear of) the United States to new heights and with Arab ruling elites more willing than ever before to defer to American foreign policy preferences, the moment seemed rich with promise and opportunity.

But the moment proved to be short-lived. Washington's decision to desist from toppling Saddam Hussein in 1991 was a prelude to a gradual, but steady, erosion of American influence in the years that followed. The defiant Iraqi dictator succeeded in turning his military defeat in 1991 into a great political achievement, making himself a symbol of resistance to American encroachment in a region that regarded the prosperous and powerful USA with much suspicion and envy. Only the determined war on terrorism launched by a new Bush administration in Afghanistan, fully ten years after Desert Storm, served to restore some (by no means all) of the influence forfeited during the 1990s.

This volume considers the momentous events of 1990–91 from three points of view: Arab, Israeli and, of course, American. Two additional essays serve as 'bookends' for these three perspectives. The book opens with an essay that offers an historical explanation for Iraq's decision to invade Kuwait. The volume concludes with a panoramic view of the Middle East ten years on.

The first chapter, by Michael T. Klare, outlines the prelude to the 1991 Gulf War. He examines events and circumstances during the first Gulf War (1980–88) between Iraq and Iran. Klare suggests that the empowerment of Iraq via the massive arms transfers along with Western – particularly American – lenience toward Saddam Hussein's regime played an important part in setting the stage for the invasion of Kuwait and the subsequent Gulf War.

Consideration of the Arab perspective begins with a chapter by F. Gregory Gause that views the events of 1990–91 as an Arab civil war. Gause discusses inter-Arab politics during the crisis, and the challenges that the war presented to the stability of the Arab regimes, the dominant concern of ruling elites. The author points out that transnational Arab identity remains a powerful force in the region's politics despite the strengthening of individual Arab states. Next, Gabriel Ben-Dor examines the conditions that enabled the Arabs to participate in the international coalition against Iraq, along with the ensuing constraints that limited the coalition's freedom of action. He also enumerates the lessons to be learnt by scholars and practitioners about the inter-Arab system.

The section dealing with Israel starts with a discussion by Efraim Inbar on Jerusalem's response to the conquest of Kuwait and its behavior during the Gulf War. The limitations on Israel's freedom of action during the war stemmed from the fact that it was a small state operating in an emerging unipolar international system. Nevertheless, Inbar argues that a counterfactual analysis of Israel's decision to refrain from retaliation to Iraqi missile attacks indicates that Israel's willingness to stay on the sidelines was highly contingent. In the next chapter, Stuart Cohen argues that the Gulf War's impact on Israeli national security thinking and defense policies was actually quite limited. At most, the 1990–91 events served to accelerate already-existing trends, namely a growing awareness of the ballistic missile threat, a shift to deterrence based on enhanced power projection capabilities, modifications in the force structure of the Israel Defense Force (IDF), and shifts in the pattern of civil–military relations.

The section on the United States begins with Thomas G. Mahnken taking US policymakers to task for ending the Gulf War prematurely. Doing so, he argues, robbed the coalition of the opportunity to translate an unequivocal battlefield victory into a durable postwar political settlement conducive both to Western interests and to regional peace and stability. Mahnken claims that beyond marching to Baghdad, a scenario rejected in Washington, several additional politico-military options existed at that time, which could have led to a political victory. The accompanying chapter in this section, by Andrew Bacevich, offers a balanced discussion of the Gulf War's impact on the United States and on US policy during the following decade. He finds that the war reaffirmed American dominance in world politics, changed American expectations regarding the nature of war, paved the way for greater American military activism in an unexpectedly orderless world, and blurred civil–military boundaries allowing for a larger, but problematic, role of the armed forces in foreign policy-making.

In the concluding chapter Efraim Karsh considers the management of the Gulf crisis, and the consequences of the war on relations in the Middle East, particularly between Israel and its neighbors. Karsh rejects the tendency to see the Gulf crisis primarily as a clash between the West and regional Muslim states, emphasizing the significant role of the regional rather than the extra-regional powers. Moreover, he argues that the Gulf War proves that statist structures remain strong and politically more attractive than the notion of an Arab nation.

This volume attempts to place the Gulf crisis of 1990–91 in historical perspective. But it is history with a purpose: a decade after the second Gulf War, few of the bright hopes of peace and harmony entertained in the immediate aftermath of Desert Storm have been fulfilled. Although this short, but turbulent, chapter in Middle Eastern history ended on a seemingly positive note, it failed to produce even a semblance of peace and stability in the region. However baffling and frustrating the region may appear, it is certain to remain a central preoccupation of American policy-makers well into the twenty-first century. In the Middle East today violence perdures – all the more reason to subject the events of 1990–91 to critical reexamination.

This volume is the outgrowth of international cooperation among several academic institutions. The Begin–Sadat (BESA) Center for Strategic Studies at Bar-Ilan University and two centers at Boston University, the Center for International Relations and the International History Institute, collaborated in organizing an international conference on 'Reassessing the Gulf War', which took place in Boston in February 2001. Most of the chapters included in this collection were initially presented at this conference. Additional essays were solicited afterwards.

We gratefully acknowledge the generous financial support of the McCormick Tribune Foundation, which made this project possible. We thank the staff of the Center for International Relations, especially Jain Yu and Emily Thompson, for making the conference a great success. We wish to thank Elisheva Brown of the BESA Center for her rigorous editing, and Hava Waxman-Koen and Alona Briner-Rozenman for their efforts in preparing this volume for publication.

Andrew J. Bacevich
Center for International Relations
Boston University

Efraim Inbar
BESA Center for
Strategic Studies
Bar-Ilan University

Part I:

Prelude to Desert Storm

1

Arms Transfers to Iran and Iraq during the Iran–Iraq War of 1980–88 and the Origins of the Gulf War

MICHAEL T. KLARE

Between 1981 and 1988, during the Iran–Iraq War, Iran and Iraq together purchased $65 billion of conventional weaponry from external sources.[1] Along with Saudi Arabia and a handful of other countries, Iran and Iraq were among the leading recipients of imported munitions during this period, jointly accounting for 22 per cent of all arms transfers to the developing world.[2] Included in the weapons supplied to Iran and Iraq during these years were many types of advanced combat systems, including fighter aircraft, attack helicopters, tanks, heavy artillery pieces and armored personnel carriers.[3] In addition, both belligerents acquired technology and materials for the manufacture of nuclear, chemical and biological weapons along with ballistic missile delivery systems. Indeed, it is hard to think of any other major conflict in which the principal belligerents were able to acquire such a wide array of weapons and technology from the outside world.

There are many aspects of the arms trade with Iran and Iraq during this period that deserve careful study. Much can be said, for example, about the political and economic arrangements devised by the two belligerents to acquire weapons from external

3

sources – in some cases, from identical sources. Likewise, much can be said about the interests and motives of the supplying countries in providing these weapons to one or both of the belligerents.[4] Of equal interest is the impact of particular arms deliveries on the conduct of the war itself. However, this chapter will concentrate on those aspects of the arms trade to Iran and Iraq in 1980–88 that had a direct bearing on the events of 1990–91.

These are:

1. **The empowerment of Iraq.** Many factors contributed to Iraq's military successes in the latter part of the Iran–Iraq War, but one of the most significant was the fact that Iraq was able to import approximately three times as much weaponry (when measured in dollar terms) during this period as was Iran.[5] Iraq was also more successful than Iran in obtaining relatively sophisticated weapons from foreign sources, giving it a further advantage in combat power. As a result, Iraq emerged from the 1980–88 conflict with a large and well-equipped military force – in fact, one of the largest and best-equipped forces in the developing world. As will be argued here, the possession of all this weaponry helped to generate the confidence with which Saddam Hussein initiated the invasion and occupation of Kuwait in August 1990.

2. **The impoverishment of Iraq.** Although massive arms purchases by Iraq in 1981–88 contributed to its battlefield successes against Iran and endowed the country with a very powerful military establishment, they also depleted the nation's treasury and forced Baghdad to borrow billions of dollars from foreign lenders. Thus, when the Iran–Iraq War ended and Iraq faced the monumental task of rebuilding its shattered infrastructure, it faced the unpleasant task of paying back its various creditors. This created significant political problems for Saddam Hussein, in that any payments he made to outside creditors would deprive him of the resources he needed to satisfy the desire of his constituents to see some benefits for their enormous sacrifices during the war itself.

4

3. **Iraq's quarrel with Kuwait.** Of Iraq's various creditors during the Iran–Iraq War, Kuwait was one of the most significant. According to some estimates, Kuwait lent Iraq some $10 billion for military purchases during the 1980–88 conflict.[6] These sums were evidently provided to Baghdad with the tacit understanding that Iraq was defending the lower Gulf Arab states against the revolutionaries in Tehran. Hence, when the war was over and Iran was defeated, Saddam Hussein had some reason to believe that the loans would be forgiven as a reward for Iraq's great sacrifices in the common struggle. When this proved *not* to be the case, Saddam became furious at the Kuwaiti leadership and began making preparations to address this problem through extraordinary and irregular means.

4. **America's embrace of Saddam Hussein.** Although the United States did not directly arm Iraq in 1980–88, it facilitated Iraq's arms buildup in several ways: by permitting its allies in the region to transfer their own US-supplied weapons to Iraq; by allowing Iraq to acquire civilian products in the United States that could be used for military purposes (such as heavy trucks and helicopters); and by awarding agricultural credits to Iraq that were used to acquire military technology. The United States also sought to discourage its allies from providing weapons to Iran – an endeavor known as Operation Staunch – while encouraging them to sell to Iraq. These moves were described at the time as expressions of a US 'tilt' towards Iraq (or, more accurately, as a desire to contain revolutionary Iran, then viewed as the greater threat to US interests in the Gulf). To what degree this led Saddam Hussein to conclude that he could invade Kuwait without risk of intervention by the United States cannot be known, but it must have been a factor in his overall calculations.

When connected, these four points suggest that arms sales to Iran and Iraq during 1980–88 played a significant role in setting the stage for the Gulf War of 1990–91. But before developing this argument further, supporting data will be provided for each of these four points.

THE EMPOWERMENT OF IRAQ

The Iran–Iraq War of 1980–88 was the longest interstate conflict of the twentieth century, and one of the bloodiest. According to conservative estimates, the two belligerents jointly suffered 367,000 dead and over 700,000 wounded during the war. Both sides also experienced substantial physical devastation, entailing the destruction of cities, roads, bridges, refineries and other forms of infrastructure. The destruction of both human life and materials was the product of a war in which both parties fought one major battle after another in an unrelenting effort to achieve a decisive victory.

At the war's onset in 1980, both belligerents possessed substantial quantities of major weapons. Iran had been a major recipient of US arms during the 1970s, under the reign of Shah Mohammed Reza Pahlavi. (This relationship was terminated in January 1980, when the Shah fled Iran and the country came under the control of radical Shi'ite clerics.) Iraq, meanwhile, had established a significant arms-supply relationship with France and the Soviet Union.[7] As a result, both parties entered the conflict with a wide array of modern combat systems – tanks, artillery, aircraft and so on. These included, for Iran, M-48, M-60 and Chieftain tanks, F-4, F-5 and F-14 fighter planes, and AH-1S helicopter gunships; for Iraq, they included T-54/55, T-62, T-72 and AMX-30 tanks, MiG-21 and MiG-23 fighters and Mi-24 helicopter gunships.[8]

Almost from the beginning, the two sides committed major forces to the military contest, producing intense battles that claimed many lives and resulted in the rapid attrition of existing arms supplies.[9] In the intense air and ground campaigns of January 1983, for example, Iraq is believed to have lost 80 combat aircraft and Iran 55.[10] To sustain the fighting, therefore, it quickly became necessary for both belligerents to obtain fresh military supplies from external sources. (Although both Iran and Iraq at that time possessed some capacity to manufacture small arms and light weapons, they lacked the capacity to manufacture tanks, aircraft and other heavy weapons.) The procurement of arms from abroad thus became a major consideration in the military planning of Iran and Iraq.[11]

The fact that both parties to the conflict required large quantities of fresh weaponry gave external suppliers considerable influence over the course of the war: by favoring one side or the other in their collective deliveries, they could help decide which belligerent would enjoy the advantage in military firepower; by denying arms to a particular belligerent, moreover, they would weaken that side's capacity to undertake major offensives. That the major suppliers, particularly the United States, France and the Soviet Union, chose to employ this leverage for their own national purposes is beyond dispute.[12]

In the early stages of the war, when Iraqi forces invaded and occupied Iranian territory and Iran sought to mobilize sufficient strength to push the Iraqis out, the major suppliers remained neutral in the conflict and refrained from major deliveries to either side. However, when Iran invaded Iraq in July 1982, the attitudes of the suppliers underwent a significant change. The United States, which feared the ascendancy of revolutionary Iran, began to aid Iraq in a variety of direct and indirect ways (Washington was also angry at Iran for the 1980 takeover of the US embassy in Tehran and the subsequent hostage crisis). France, which had established close ties with Saddam Hussein – and was owed considerable sums for the transfer of weaponry – sought to bolster Iraqi defenses. And the Soviet Union, which also feared the aggressive posture of Iran, joined the United States and France in aiding Iraq. A number of other suppliers (including Israel and North Korea) chose to align with Iran at this time, but Iraq became the principal beneficiary of external arms flows.[13]

Over the eight-year course of the war, both the United States and the Soviet Union chose to supply Iran with weapons at certain moments. In Washington's case, this was part of an attempt in 1985 to win the release of US hostages in Lebanon and to curry favor with (supposedly) moderate clerics in Tehran – an initiative known to us today as the Iran-Contra Affair.[14] Similarly, Moscow sought to gain favor with Iran's new rulers early in the conflict.[15] Nevertheless, both superpowers favored Iraq over the long haul, providing Baghdad with the bulk of the

arms and military assistance they provided to the two belligerents during the conflict.

The results of these various arms-supply arrangements are
clearly evident in Table 1. Between 1981 and 1988, Iraq received
77 per cent of the arms delivered to the two belligerents (in
dollar terms), while Iran received only 23 per cent. This imbalance greatly favored Iraq during the later stages of the war, when
Iraqi forces possessed overwhelming superiority in aircraft,
tanks, heavy artillery and missiles. Iran tried to compensate for
its disadvantage in combat arms by employing human-wave
attacks against Iraqi positions, but this often resulted in horrific
casualty rates and gradually eroded Iran's capacity and willingness to continue the fighting.[16]

Not so readily evident from the figures in Table 1 is another
important feature of the arms trade with Iran and Iraq: the fact
that Iraq was much more successful than Iran in gaining access
to relatively sophisticated weapons. During the course of the
war, Iraq was able to procure late-model aircraft, missiles, tanks
and artillery pieces from the Soviet Union and France, while
Iran had to content itself with less-sophisticated variants from

Table 1:
Arms Transfers to Iran and Iraq in 1981–88 (in millions of current US$)

Supplier	Iran		Iraq	
	Orders	Deliveries*	Orders	Deliveries*
Soviet Union	240	370	20,650	21,370
China	3,970	2,750	5,520	4,380
Other Communist	5,740	4,550	6,030	6,300
European Non-Communist	5,340	4,170	9,790	10,710
Other Non-Communist	2,190	1,970	5,260	3,900
Total	17,480	13,810	47,250	46,660

Source: Richard F. Grimmett, *Trends in Conventional Arms Transfers to the Third World by
Major Supplier, 1981–1988* (Washington, DC: Congressional Research Service, 1989).

Note: *Deliveries usually follow orders by a year or more, so the two columns are not
identical.

Table 2:
Iraq's Inventory of Major Conventional Arms, 1980 and 1990

Category	1980	1990
Combat aircraft	12 Tu-22 10 Il-28 80 MiG-23B 60 Su-7B 30 Su-20 115 MiG-21 15 Hunter (Total: 322)	8 Tu-16 8 Tu-22 94 Mirage F-1EQ, F-1EQ5 18 MiG-29 25 MiG-25 70 MiG-23BN 70 MiG-21 30 Su-7 50 Su-20 30 Su-25 120 Chinese J-6, J-7 (Total: 523)
Main battle tanks	1,700 T-54, T-55, T-62 100 T-34 (Total: 1,800)	2,500 T-54, T-55, M-77 1,500 Chinese T-59, T-69 1,000 T-62 500 T-72 30 Chieftain (Total: 5,530)
Armored personnel carriers	estimated 1,700	estimated 8,100
Heavy artillery pieces	estimated 930	estimated 3,500

Source: International Institute for Strategic Studies (IISS), The Military Balance (London: IISS), editions for 1979–80 and 1989–90.

China and North Korea.[17] Thus, while Iran's inventory of major combat systems gradually shrank during the eight years of fighting (from 447 operational combat aircraft to 70, and from 1,735 tanks to 500), Iraq's actually grew during this period (from 322 aircraft to 523, and from 1,800 tanks to 5,530).[18] (See Table 2.)

Of particular significance in this regard were the French sales to Iraq of 5 Super-Etendard fighter-bombers and 90 Mirage F-1 combat planes, all of which came equipped with a variety of sophisticated air-to-air and air-to-ground missiles (including Exocet anti-shipping missiles). In addition, the Soviet Union supplied Iraq with late-model MiG fighters. Meanwhile, Iran was largely unable to employ the advanced aircraft it had received from the United States in the 1970s because of its inability to obtain the necessary spare parts (due to the US arms embargo on

Iran), enabling Iraq's acquisition of advanced aircraft from France and the Soviet Union to dominate the airspace over the battlefield and to attack cities, military installations and oil facilities deep within Iranian territory.[19]

Of equal significance was Iraq's superior access to ballistic missiles and chemical-warfare (CW) technology. Owing to its close ties with the Soviet Union, Iraq was able to acquire a significant number of Scud-B ballistic missiles during the course of the war, including a delivery of 300 in 1986.[20] Baghdad also developed its own missile-production capability using know-how and equipment obtained from Western sources.[21] By contrast, Iran was only able to obtain a small number of missiles, primarily from North Korea. This imbalance allowed Iraq to fire far more missiles at targets in Iran than Iran was able to fire at Iraq. In 1988, for example, Iraq fired 189 Scuds at Iran while Iran fired only 52 at Iraq. Although these weapons caused relatively little physical damage, they produced great anxiety among the civilian population and thus (along with the heavy casualties produced by human-wave attacks) eroded Iran's determination to continue the fighting.[22]

The fact that Iraq could strike cities in Iran with long-range missiles was the source of particular concern to the Iranians because of Iraq's widespread use of chemical weapons on the battlefield. Although the Iraqis chose not to load chemical warheads on the Scuds fired at Iranian cities, they did use CW agents in attacks on Iranian ground troops and, in several well-documented cases, against civilians in Kurdish-controlled towns.[23] These agents were manufactured at CW plants in Iraq, but much of the technology involved was acquired – through deceit or otherwise – from chemical firms in Europe.[24] Here, too, Iraq enjoyed an advantage over Iran: although Iran also began to manufacture chemical agents during the later stages of the war, its CW production capacity was much inferior to that enjoyed by Iraq.[25] (Iraq also invested considerable resources in the development of a nuclear-weapons capability at this time, but the broad scope of this effort did not become known until after the Gulf War of 1991, when UN inspectors visited Iraqi nuclear sites.[26])

As the Iran–Iraq War drew to a close in 1987 and 1988, Iraq assumed the offensive on all major fronts and achieved major successes against Iranian forces. In preparation for these battles, Baghdad acquired large quantities of basic combat gear, including tanks, armored personnel carriers, anti-tank missiles and artillery pieces.[27] Although some of these systems were lost in the final battles of the war, most were still in operating condition when the war ended on 8 August 1988. Thus, when Saddam Hussein began to consider military action against Kuwait, he was in possession of a truly massive military arsenal, unquestionably one of the largest and most advanced in the developing world. (See Table 2.)

Exactly what considerations figured in Saddam Hussein's mental calculations regarding the decision to invade Kuwait on 2 August 1990 can never be known with any degree of certainty. Obviously, many factors entered into the equation.[28] But there is no doubt that Iraq's possession of a large and powerful military arsenal was a significant element in Saddam's thinking at that time. In several speeches given in the spring and summer of 1990, he openly boasted of Iraq's military might – most notably in his Revolution Day address of 17 July 1990.[29]

The confidence-boosting effect of Iraq's military strength also figured in American analyses of Saddam's outlook. 'While the [Iran–Iraq] war brought great destruction,' then Secretary of Defense Richard Cheney observed in December 1990, 'it also left Saddam with a war-hardened military force – disciplined, organized, and tough.' Moreover, 'the country's [oil] wealth has been diverted to wage war, develop nuclear and other special weapons programs [i.e. chemical and biological weapons], commit aggression, and fuel Saddam's dreams of power and domination'. And it was against this backdrop, Cheney noted, that Saddam 'became increasingly vocal about [his disagreements with] the oil and financial policies of the other Arab states of the Gulf '.[30]

The definitive assessment of Saddam's deliberations on the eve of the 1990 invasion of Kuwait will have to await the labor of future historians. But this author is in no doubt that the possession of such a large inventory of modern weapons, along with ballistic missiles and chemical weapons, significantly contributed to Saddam's overarching sense of confidence in ordering the 2 August attack.

11

THE IMPOVERISHMENT OF IRAQ

The acquisition of so many modern weapons in the 1980s was an obvious source of strength for Iraq. But this asset did not come without a substantial cost: according to the Congressional Research Service (CRS) of the US Library of Congress, Iraq spent some $47 billion on imported weapons between 1981 and 1988, or approximately $6 billion per year (in current, uninflated dollars).[31] Although seemingly small when compared to the current US military budget of approximately $300 billion (in 2000), this amount represented a very substantial outlay for the Iraqi government. The economic impact of this outlay was even more significant given the decline in Iraq's revenues from oil exports (its main source of hard currency), which dropped from approximately $26 billion in 1980 to under $10 billion per year once the fighting began.[32] With Iraq's total war-related costs exceeding $1 billion per month,[33] it is clear that the country's arms-import expense represented a significant strain on the economy.

Lacking sufficient funds of its own, and determined to acquire as many weapons as it needed, the Iraqi government borrowed heavily from sympathetic sources – notably France, Kuwait, Saudi Arabia, the Soviet Union and the United Arab Emirates (UAE) – in order to finance the import of arms. According to Richard Cheney, Iraq borrowed $60 billion during the 1980s for military purposes.[34] These loans were not expected to be repaid while the war was still under way, but were scheduled to fall due once the fighting came to a halt.[35] Thus, when the war ended on 8 August 1988 and Iraq began the mammoth task of rebuilding its shattered infrastructure and economy, it faced the unenviable prospect of having to pay off $60 billion in outstanding loans.

The potential hardship involved in the repayment of these loans was further compounded by the devastation experienced by Iraq during the war with Iran. According to some estimates, Iraq suffered wartime losses of over $100 billion, much of which represented damage to its oil industry.[36] With his constituents now expecting some rewards for their wartime sacrifices,

Saddam Hussein desperately needed to rebuild the country's shattered infrastructure and accelerate economic activity. To do this, however, he would have to borrow more money – lots of it. But the Arab oil states were no longer willing to loan Iraq large sums of money, and other lenders were nervous about Baghdad's existing debt burden.[37] On top of this, the price of oil (Iraq's main export) had dropped significantly as a result of elevated production by Kuwait, Saudi Arabia and the UAE.[38] As a result, Baghdad faced a severe financial crisis at the very moment that it expected to reap the fruits of victory.

One aspect of this crisis deserves particular mention: the problem of reintegrating ex-soldiers into Iraq's civilian economy. No doubt most Iraqis – especially the one million men in uniform – assumed that peace with Iran would be followed by the whole-sale demobilization of Iraqi forces. With the oil industry in sham-bles, however, the Iraqi economy was in no position to absorb an additional one million new workers. Thus, any mass demobiliza-tion of Iraqi soldiers would have produced massive unemployment and political unrest. To forestall this, Saddam Hussein settled on what must have seemed the only practical solution: to keep the soldiers in uniform and maintain a warlike environment.[39]

IRAQ'S QUARREL WITH KUWAIT

By the beginning of 1990, Saddam Hussein was facing an increasingly severe economic crisis at home. Although oil pro-duction had increased, low international prices deprived Iraq of the revenues needed to rebuild its economy. What little income could be derived from oil exports was needed to sustain the bloated military establishment and to pay off foreign loans. On top of this, foreign lenders, including fraternal Arab states, could not be persuaded to provide fresh loans for economic recon-struction. Rather than address these problems by cutting gov-ernment spending and reducing the size of the military – moves that would have undercut his popularity and risked mass unrest – Saddam chose to seek recompense from his neighbors, especially Kuwait.[40]

In the months preceding the Iraqi invasion of Kuwait, Saddam Hussein charged the Kuwaitis with many crimes against the Iraqi people. These included (but were not limited to) charges that the Kuwaitis had: (1) consistently exceeded their OPEC production quotas, thereby driving down the price of oil and depriving Iraq of desperately needed funds; (2) systematically stolen oil from Iraq's Rumaila oilfield by pumping oil from the field's southern tip (which protruded into Kuwaiti territory); and (3) occupied portions of Iraqi territory.[41] But what Saddam claimed was Kuwait's greatest sin was its unwillingness to forgive the $10 billion or so that Kuwait had loaned Iraq during the Iran–Iraq War for the purchase of arms.[42]

In Saddam's view, Kuwait (like Saudi Arabia and the UAE) had loaned Iraq billions of dollars during the war with Iran out of a belief that the Iraqis were fighting not only in their own defense, but also on behalf of other Arab states that faced a threat from revolutionary Iran. Saddam's argument with the other Arab states, as summarized by Lawrence Freedman and Efraim Karsh, was phrased as follows:

> The war was not Iraq's private business … but rather a defense of the eastern flank of the Arab world against fundamentalist Iran. While the Gulf states were not asked to pay with rivers of blood for the protection of their own security, since Iraq did that on their behalf, they could not expect to take a 'free ride' on Iraq's heroic struggle.[43]

And, indeed, there is every reason to believe that Kuwait and the other Gulf states loaned the money to Iraq with their own security interests in mind.[44] The Kuwaitis, in particular, were fearful of Iranian intentions, especially after 1986, when Iran occupied the Fao Peninsula and used it as a base for launching Chinese-made HY-2 'Silkworm' missiles at oil installations in Kuwait.[45]

However, the conditions that prompted Kuwait to lend money to Iraq in 1980–88 disappeared with the end of the Iran–Iraq War, and after that Kuwait's leaders showed no inclination to absolve Iraq of its obligation to pay back the wartime loans. This stance evidently infuriated Saddam Hussein, who

14

employed increasingly harsh and threatening language in his comments on Iraq's relations with Kuwait and the other Gulf nations. At a meeting of the Arab Co-operation Council in Amman in February 1990, Saddam asked President Mubarak of Egypt and King Hussein of Jordan to inform the Gulf states that they must agree to a complete moratorium of Iraq's wartime loans and provide Baghdad with fresh economic assistance. 'Let the Gulf regimes know', he said, 'that if they do not give this money to me, I will know how to get it.'[46] This message was repeated on several occasions during the spring of 1990, but it did not alter the outlook of the Kuwaitis, who continued to insist on full repayment of the wartime loans.[47]

Saddam's quarrel with Kuwait over the wartime loans came to a head in July 1990. Claiming that the Kuwaitis' refusal to cancel the debt, cease their theft of Iraqi oil from the Rumaila oilfield and provide additional assistance to Iraq constituted the equivalent of 'military aggression' against Iraq, he called on them to make immediate concessions to Baghdad.[48] These demands were accompanied by explicit threats of violence: 'If words fail to afford us protection,' he noted on 17 July, 'we will have no choice but to resort to effective action to put things right and ensure the restitution of our rights.'[49] By this point, Iraqi forces were already mobilizing near the Kuwaiti border in apparent preparation for an attack. Still, the Kuwaitis refused to make any significant concessions, and, on 1 August, Saddam gave the orders for a full-scale invasion.

AMERICA'S EMBRACE OF SADDAM HUSSEIN

At the point of decision, when Saddam Hussein had to choose between launching the invasion of Kuwait and sending his troops back to their barracks, he had to weigh the potential gains against possible losses. Not one to take risks needlessly, Saddam would have never given the green light to an invasion if he believed that the costs would be excessive. In this case, he did not have to worry about Kuwaiti military strength, as he had with Iran: Kuwait's army, in 1990, numbered some 20,300 soldiers, or about one-fiftieth of Iraq's total troop strength.[50] What he *did* have to worry about was the possibility of counter-attack by the major powers, led by the United States. Had he truly believed that such a response was likely, Saddam would never have given the order to invade Kuwait. It is only because he determined that the risk of a counterattack was very low that he decided to go ahead. And so it is important to ask whether US behavior *prior to* August 1990 helped him reach this conclusion.

It is the belief of this author that US behavior during the Iran–Iraq War and immediately afterwards led Saddam Hussein to believe that the United States would acquiesce to the Iraqi occupation of Kuwait. This does not imply that US officials *intended* to give Saddam this impression. Had they realized that their actions would have this ultimate effect, the US leaders would have surely behaved differently. But this outcome does not seem to have been given serious consideration by White House officials (whose deliberations on Iraq have been made public[51]), and so they acted in a way that must have appeared to Saddam as reflecting a policy of appeasement.

This policy was known in Washington as the 'tilt' toward Iraq, meaning that the United States favored the success of Iraq rather than Iran in their mutual struggle, and was prepared to provide various forms of assistance to ensure that this would be the final outcome. The decision to 'tilt' in Baghdad's direction was first taken by the Reagan administration in mid-1982, when Iranian forces assumed the offensive and crossed into Iraqi territory. Although Iraq had until then been viewed in Washington as a hostile state because of its ties to Moscow and opposition to Israel, senior administration officials determined that it would be necessary to bolster the Iraqis lest they be defeated by Iran.[52] Thus, in a 1983 memo to special presidential envoy Donald Rumsfeld, William Eagleton (then head of the US Interests Section in Baghdad) affirmed that the US government 'would regard any major reversal of Iraq's fortunes as a strategic defeat of the West', and so was prepared to assist the Iraqis in a variety of ways.[53]

Concluding, then, that 'the enemy of our enemy is our friend' (to quote one former CIA official involved in these deliberations[54]), the White House took a number of steps to strengthen Iraq in its struggle against Iran. These included: (1) the provision of credit guaranties by the Agriculture Department's Commodity Credit Corporation (CCC) for the purchase by Iraq of American agricultural products (thereby freeing up Iraqi funds for military purchases); (2) the secret handover of sensitive intelligence information on Iranian military positions (much of it gleaned from satellite photography); (3) the sale to Iraq of American 'dual-use' items with obvious military applications, such as transport planes, helicopters, heavy trucks and scientific gear; and (4) the transfer to Iraq of weapons given by the United States to its allies in the region, including Egypt, Jordan, Kuwait and Saudi Arabia.[55]

Cumulatively speaking, these actions represented a significant boost to Iraq's overall military capability. Between 1983 and 1990, the CCC guaranteed $5 billion in commercial loans made to Iraq for the purchase of US agricultural products, most of which were never paid back. These loans enabled Iraq to feed its population (and its troops) throughout the war period, and to use its other sources of income (whether from oil sales or unrestricted loans by friendly governments) to purchase military equipment.[56] It is also believed that Iraq used some of these loans to purchase arms and military-related equipment, including hardware used in the manufacture of weapons of mass destruction.[57]

The delivery of US intelligence information also constituted a major asset to Iraq in its war against Iran. This data reportedly included satellite imagery of Iranian troop deployments in the major battle zones, allowing Baghdad to anticipate the timing and location of Iranian offensives and thus to concentrate its defensive forces in the most advantageous positions. Originally, such information was given to King Hussein of Jordan for delivery to Saddam Hussein, but eventually US intelligence officials were stationed in Baghdad in order to facilitate the delivery of strategic data.[58] (Although originally intended to assist Iraq in repelling Iranian attacks, this intelligence-sharing program was continued through the end of the war and in the period that followed, ending only months before the Iraqi invasion of Kuwait.[59])

17

No less significant was the delivery to Iraq of dual-use equipment with obvious military applications. These deliveries apparently began in May 1982, when the Commerce Department approved the sale of six Lockheed L-100 cargo planes (the civilian version of the Air Force's C-130 transport).[60] This was followed, in December 1982, by the sale of 60 Hughes 500MD scout helicopters to Iraq.[61] Fourteen months later, Secretary of State George Shultz approved the sale of 2,000 heavy trucks to Iraq in a deal worth an estimated $224 million.[62] In agreeing to the transfer of these, and other such items, American officials were fully aware that the Iraqis would use them in the war effort against Iran; indeed, this was the very purpose of the US sales program.[63]

Finally, the United States permitted the retransfer to Iraq of US arms given or sold to its regional allies, including Egypt, Jordan, Kuwait and Saudi Arabia. These munitions included UH-1 'Huey' helicopters transferred from Jordan, TOW anti-tank missiles from Kuwait and Mk-84 bombs from Saudi Arabia. Although retransfers of this sort were illegal under US law, the Reagan administration gave its tacit approval to these deliveries.[64]

In addition to these purely military (or military-related) actions, the United States also made certain *symbolic* gestures to Iraq that were highly significant in terms of conferring US approval on the Baghdad regime. In some sense, these actions were even more important than the military gestures, in that they allowed Saddam Hussein to conduct his military buildup with the apparent blessing of the US government.

The first of these gestures was the February 1982 decision by the Reagan administration to remove Iraq from the list of countries accused of supporting international terrorism. Taking this step was the necessary prelude to the other actions described above, as US law prohibited the delivery of any form of aid to countries named on the list. In fact, US officials were well aware in 1982 that Baghdad continued to harbor noted terrorists like Abu Nidal, but this was considered less important than assisting Iraq at a time when Iran appeared to be winning the war.[65]

Even more significant was the administration's decision to turn a blind eye to the widespread use of chemical weapons by

Iraqi forces. Iraq began using lethal CW agents on a significant scale in December 1982, in order to blunt Iranian human-wave attacks on front-line positions; by mid 1983, these weapons were being used on a regular basis.[66] Top US officials learnt of Iraq's use of chemical weapons in this fashion no later than November 1983. In a memorandum dated 11 November 1983, the Department of State confirmed the 'almost daily use of CW' by Iraq.[67] Despite this fact, Donald Rumsfeld flew to Baghdad on 17 December 1983 and told Tariq Aziz and Saddam Hussein that the United States was prepared to restore diplomatic relations (severed since the Six-Day War of 1967) and to provide Iraq with agricultural credits and other forms of assistance.[68]

Diplomatic relations were formally restored on 26 November 1984 and the United States continued to aid Iraq in the aforementioned ways despite continuing reports of Iraqi CW use. Nor was US aid terminated after it was reported that Iraq had used chemical weapons against Kurdish civilians in the town of Halabja in March 1988, causing an estimated 5,000 deaths. At no time did President Reagan or Vice-President Bush speak out in condemnation of Iraqi CW use, or in any way indicate that Washington opposed such action.[69] In an internal memorandum, the Department of State noted that 'the failure of the international community to mobilize an effective response [to the CW attack on Halabja] has lowered the inhibitions on CW use and may have conferred a measure of legitimacy on the use of these weapons in the region'.[70] Under these circumstances, it is reasonable to assume that Saddam Hussein came to view the United States as fundamentally disinclined to challenge his more egregious behavior.

The same can be said of the US reaction to the Iraqi missile attack on the USS *Stark*, on 17 May 1987. This attack, made by a French-supplied Mirage F-1EQ aircraft equipped with Exocet missiles, resulted in the loss of 37 American lives. But despite the fact that Baghdad never provided a credible explanation for the action (blaming it entirely on pilot error), the United States took no steps to punish Iraq for the deed, which it surely would have done if the attack had been made by an Iranian plane. In fact, Washington chose this moment to step up its pressure on

Tehran (mainly by defending Saudi and Kuwaiti tankers in the Gulf against Iranian naval attacks), thereby aiding Iraq in its war against Iran.[71] This, too, must have led Saddam Hussein to view the United States as an especially forgiving ally.

All of these behaviors can, of course, be justified in the name of *realpolitik*, out of the need to protect vital US interests against the greater danger of Iran. But whether intended or not, US support for Iraq during the Iran–Iraq War established a bond with Saddam Hussein that Washington was loath to break when the war came to an end. So, despite mounting evidence that Iraq was expanding its CW capability and developing nuclear weapons,[72] the United States continued in 1989–90 to provide Iraq with various forms of aid, including intelligence information and CCC credit guaranties.[73] This policy was confirmed on 2 October 1989, when President George Bush (the elder) signed a national security directive (NSD-26) calling for closer relations between the United States and Iraq.[74]

As 1989 gave way to 1990, some elements of the US leadership began to doubt the wisdom of maintaining such close ties with an authoritarian dictator, especially after Saddam Hussein made threatening statements toward Israel and Kuwait and accelerated the development of nuclear weapons. But despite growing concern over Iraqi behavior, the Bush administration never rescinded NSD-26 or signaled its intent to sever its ties with Saddam Hussein. From Saddam's perspective, therefore, the United States remained the forgiving ally he had become accustomed to dealing with during the Iran–Iraq War. And so it is this author's view that Saddam attacked Kuwait in the belief – mistaken, as it turned out – that Washington would continue to overlook his aggressive acts.

CONCLUSION

For most Americans, the Gulf War began on 2 August 1990, with the Iraqi invasion of Kuwait, and was driven largely by Saddam Hussein's megalomaniacal pursuit of power. And, of course, this is one way to perceive the conflict. As this chapter attempts to show, however, the Gulf War was in many respects an outgrowth of the Iran–Iraq War, and cannot be fully understood without examining its ties to that earlier event.

The sale of arms to Iraq during the Iran–Iraq War furnished many of the key ingredients for the 1990–91 Gulf conflict: the *means* (all of the munitions supplied to Iraq); the *motive* (a desire to eliminate the burden of paying for all those arms); the intended *victim* (Kuwait); and the necessary international *setting* (a consistent pattern of US acquiescence to Iraqi misbehavior). This may not represent a *complete* explanation of the 1990–91 Gulf conflict, but it goes a long way toward explaining what otherwise appears so inexplicable – Iraq's seemingly self-destructive invasion of Kuwait on 2 August 1990. It seems that only by considering these factors is it possible to place this momentous event in its proper perspective.

NOTES

1. Richard F. Grimmett, *Trends in Conventional Arms Transfers to the Third World by Major Supplier, 1981–1988* (Washington, DC: Congressional Research Service, Library of Congress, 4 August 1989), pp. 40–1. Figures are in then-current US dollars.
2. Ibid., p. 33.
3. For details on these transfers, see Stockholm International Peace Research Institute (SIPRI), *SIPRI Yearbook 1989* (Oxford: Oxford University Press, 1989), pp. 252–4. See also prior editions of this work.
4. For background, see Anthony H. Cordesman and Abraham R. Wagner, *The Lessons of Modern War*, Vol. II: *The Iran–Iraq War* (Boulder, CO: Westview Press, 1990), pp. 45–53, 120–2, 156–9, 162–5, 168–9, 232–3, 358–61.
5. According to the CRS, Iraq received $47.7 billion of arms from outside sources in 1981–88, compared to only $13.8 billion for Iran. See Grimmett, *Trends in Conventional Arms Transfers*, pp. 50–1.
6. Lawrence Freedman and Efraim Karsh, *The Gulf Conflict 1990–1991* (Princeton, NJ: Princeton University Press, 1993), p. 41.
7. For background on these arms-supply arrangements, see Andrew J. Pierre, *The Global Politics of Arms Sales* (Princeton, NJ: Princeton University Press, 1982), pp. 84, 14–54, 193–7. On US sales to Iran, see also Michael T. Klare, *American Arms Supermarket* (Austin, TX: University of Texas Press, 1985), pp. 108–26.
8. International Institute for Srategic Studies (IISS), *The Military Balance, 1979–80* (London: IISS, 1979), pp. 39–40.
9. On the opening stages of the war, see Cordesman and Wagner, *Lessons of Modern War*, Chaps 4–6. See also Dilip Hiro, *The Longest War: The Iran–Iraq Military Conflict* (New York: Routledge, 1991).
10. Cordesman and Wagner, *Lessons of Modern War*, p. 158.
11. For discussion, see ibid., pp. 156–9, 162.

21

12. For discussion, see ibid., pp. 48–53, 102–5, 156–9. See also Tirman, *Spoils of War: The Human Cost of American Arms Trade* (New York: Free Press, 1997), pp. 98–111.
13. See Cordesman and Wagner, *Lessons of Modern War*, pp. 48–53, 102–5; Hiro, *The Longest War*, pp. 114–28. On French and Soviet deliveries to Iraq, see Kenneth R. Timmerman, *The Death Lobby: How the West Armed Iraq* (Boston, MA: Houghton Mifflin, 1991), Chaps 1–4.
14. For background, see Cordesman and Wagner, *Lessons of Modern War*, pp. 237–42.
15. See Hiro, *The Longest War*, pp. 72–4.
16. For discussion, see Cordesman and Wagner, *Lessons of Modern War*, pp. 357–61, 431–3.
17. For an inventory of arms transfers to Iran and Iraq during this period, see *SIPRI Yearbook 1989*, pp. 252–4.
18. This data was obtained by comparing the 1979–80 edition of *The Military Balance* (see n. 8) with the 1989–90 edition.
19. See Cordesman and Wagner, *Lessons of Modern War*, pp. 156–9, 208–13, 242–4. On French arms sales to Iraq, see Timmerman, *The Death Lobby*, pp. 90–5, 108–9, 136–8, 230–1.
20. Cordesman and Wagner, *Lessons of Modern War*, p. 364.
21. For background on the Iraqi missile effort, see Timmerman, *The Death Lobby*, pp. 157–60, 204–7, 253–7, 267–70, 288, 290–3.
22. See Cordesman and Wagner, *Lessons of Modern War*, pp. 363–8, 495–503.
23. Ibid., pp. 513–18.
24. For background on Iraq's CW production effort, see ibid., pp. 506–12. On the role of Western technology in this effort, see Timmerman, *The Death Lobby*, pp. 103–12, 131–5, 148. On French and German sales of CW-related technology to Iraq, see Youssef M. Ibrahim, 'French Reportedly Sent Iraq Chemical War Tools', *New York Times*, 21 September 1990; R. Jeffrey Smith and Marc Fisher, 'Germans Prime Iraq's War Machine', *Washington Post*, 23 July 1992.
25. For background and discussion, see Cordesman and Wagner, *Lessons of Modern War*, pp. 506–18.
26. For background on the Iraqi nuclear weapons program, see Rodney W. Jones and Mark G. McDonough, *Tracking Nuclear Proliferation* (Washington, DC: Carnegie Endowment for International Peace, 1998), pp. 187–204.
27. On the Iranian buildup and the final battles of the war, see Cordesman and Wagner, *Lessons of Modern War*, pp. 353–411; Hiro, *The Longest War*, pp. 167–240.
28. For discussion of these considerations, see Freedman and Karsh, *The Gulf Conflict*, pp. 19–63. See also Walid Khalidi, 'Iraq vs. Kuwait: Claims and Counterclaims', in Micah L. Sifry and Christopher Cerf (eds), *The Gulf War Reader* (New York: Times Books, 1991), pp. 57–65.
29. For a discussion of this speech and others by Saddam, see 'Kuwait, How the West Blundered', *Economist*, 23 September 1990, pp. 19–21.
30. US Congress, Senate, Committee on Armed Services, *Crisis in the Persian Gulf Region: US Policy Options and Implications*, Hearings before the Committee on Armed Services, 101st Cong., 2nd Session, 1990, p. 652.
31. Grimmett, *Trends in Conventional Arms Transfers*, p. 41.
32. Cordesman and Wagner, *Lessons of Modern War*, pp. 185–6.
33. Ibid., p. 135.
34. Senate Committee on Armed Services, *Crisis in the Persian Gulf*, p. 652.
35. For background on Saudi and Kuwaiti loans to Iraq, see Hiro, *The Longest War*, pp. 75–7, 114–15.
36. Cordesman and Wagner, *Lessons of Modern War*, p. 2.
37. See Freedman and Karsh, *The Gulf Conflict*, pp. 37–9.
38. This was one of Saddam Hussein's major complaints against his Arab neighbors in 1990. See ibid., pp. 45–50. See also Khalidi, 'Iraq vs. Kuwait', p. 63.
39. See Freedman and Karsh, *The Gulf Conflict*, p. 30. See also Mike Blakely, 'The

Persian Gulf', in Michael E. Brown and Richard N. Rosecrance (eds), *The Cost of Conflict* (Lanham, MD: Rowman and Littlefield, 1999), p. 112.

40. This analysis is based on Freedman and Karsh, *The Gulf Conflict*, pp. 42–50.
41. These grievances are summarized in Khalidi, 'Iraq vs. Kuwait', pp. 61–4. See also Freedman and Karsh, *The Gulf Conflict*, pp. 42–7.
42. For discussion of these charges, see Freedman and Karsh, *The Gulf Conflict*, pp. 42–63; Khalidi, 'Iraq vs. Kuwait', pp. 57–65.
43. Freedman and Karsh, *The Gulf Conflict*, p. 45.
44. See Hiro, *The Longest War*, pp. 76–7, 114–16, 155–6.
45. On Iran's occupation of Fao and Kuwait's reaction, see ibid., pp. 167–86, 213–15. On the Silkworm attacks, see Cordesman and Wagner, *Lessons of Modern War*, pp. 328–41.
46. Quoted in Freedman and Karsh, *The Gulf Conflict*, p. 45.
47. Ibid., pp. 45–7.
48. This position was outlined in a memorandum signed by Tariq Aziz, Iraq's Foreign Minister, and given to Chadly Klibi, Secretary-General of the Arab League, on 16 July 1990. For summary, see ibid., pp. 47–8.
49. From Saddam's Revolution Day speech of 17 July 1990, as quoted in ibid., pp. 48–9.
50. *The Military Balance 1989–1990*, pp. 101, 104.
51. See the documents collected by the National Security Archive and summarized in Joyce Battle (ed.), *Iraqgate: Saddam Hussein, US Policy, and the Prelude to the Persian Gulf War (1980–1994)* (Washington, DC: National Security Archive, 1995).
52. For background on the US decision to aid Iraq at this time, see Alan Friedman, *Spider's Web: The Secret History of How the White House Illegally Armed Iraq* (New York: Bantam Books, 1993), Chaps 1–3, 8. See also Freedman and Karsh, *The Gulf Conflict*, pp. 24–5; Seymour M. Hersh, 'US Secretly Gave Aid to Iraq Early in Its War Against Iran', *New York Times*, 26 January 1992; Hiro, *The Longest War*, pp. 119–21.
53. US Department of State cable, 'Talking Points for Amb. Rumsfeld's Meeting with Tariq Aziz and Saddam Hussein', 14 December 1983. Document supplied to the National Security Archive under the Freedom of Information Act.
54. Edward Juchniewicz, as quoted in William Scott Malone, 'Like Playing Poker with Our Cards Face Up: How the US Gave its Secrets to Saddam Hussein', *Washington Post National Weekly Edition*, 11–17 November 1991, p. 22.
55. For background on these initiatives, see Joyce Battle, 'Friends in Deed: The United States and Iraq Before the Persian Gulf War', in Battle, *Iraqgate*, pp. 19–23.
56. On the CCC program, see Friedman, *Spider's Web*, pp. 94–108, 112; Timmerman, *The Death Lobby*, pp. 126–7, 131, 196, 225–6, 260.
57. A significant share of the CCC credits were funneled through the Atlanta branch of the Banca Nazionale del Lavoro (BNL), a large international bank owned by the Italian government. Federal prosecutors later charged BNL's Atlanta branch officers with illegally supplying Iraq with loans for the purchase of military-related equipment. For background on the BNL-Atlanta scandal, see Peter Mantius, *Shell Game* (New York: St Martin's Press, 1995). See also Timmerman, *The Death Lobby*, pp. 195–7, 225–8, 285–7. On the use of CCC funds to purchase arms in other countries, see Dean Baquet, 'Documents Charge Prewar Iraq Swap: US Food for Arms', *New York Times*, 27 April 1992.
58. For background on this effort, see Friedman, *Spider's Web*, pp. 27–8, 31–3, 36; Bernard Gwertzman, 'Iraq Gets Reports from US for War with Iran', *New York Times*, 16 December 1986; Hersh, 'US Secretly Gave Aid to Iraq'.
59. 'US Gave Data to Iraq 3 Months Before Invasion', *Los Angeles Times*, 10 March 1992.
60. Associated Press wire story, 18 December 1982.
61. Timmerman, *The Death Lobby*, pp. 122–3.
62. US Department of State, 'Briefing to Sen. Boschwitz on Truck Sales to Iraq,

February 14, 1984'. Document supplied to the National Security Archive under the Freedom of Information Act.

63. Ibid. For discussion, see Battle, 'Friends in Deed'.
64. See Friedman, *Spider's Web*, pp. 17, 33; Hersh, 'US Secretly Gave Aid to Iraq'.
65. See Battle, 'Friends in Deed', p. 19; Friedman, *Spider's Web*, pp. 8, 12, 19, 25–6, 93–4.
66. Cordesman and Wagner, *Lessons of Modern War*, pp. 513–14.
67. US Department of State Memorandum, 'Iraq Use of Chemical Weapons', 11 November 1983. Document supplied to the National Security Archive under the Freedom of Information Act.
68. US Congress, *United States–Iraqi Relations* (Washington, DC: Congressional Research Service, US Library of Congress, 30 July 1986), p. 14. See also Friedman, *Spider's Web*, p. 28.
69. On Halabja, see Cordesman and Wagner, *Lessons of Modern War*, pp. 370, 517; Timmerman, *The Death Lobby*, p. 293.
70. US Department of State, 'US Policy toward Iraqi CW Use', Memorandum to the Secretary of State, 13 November 1988. Document supplied to the National Security Archive under the Freedom of Information Act.
71. For background on the *Stark* affair and the events that followed, see Cordesman and Wagner, *Lessons of Modern War*, pp. 282–92, 295–302, 549–58.
72. In an assessment of the BNL-Atlanta scandal (see n. 57), for example, the CIA reported at length on Iraq's clandestine weapons of mass destruction (WMD) programs. See Central Intelligence Agency, 'Iraq–Italy: Repercussions of the BNL-Atlanta Scandal', 6 November 1989. Document supplied to the National Security Archive under the Freedom of Information Act.
73. For discussion of this period, see Battle, 'Friends in Deed', pp. 20–1; Freedman and Karsh, *The Gulf Conflict*, pp. 23–8; Friedman, *Spider's Web*, pp. 131–64.
74. Specifically, NSD-26 determined that 'Normal relations between the United States and Iraq would serve our longer-term interests in both the Gulf and the Middle East. The United States Government should propose economic and political incentives for Iraq to moderate its behavior and to increase our influence with Iraq.' US National Security Council, National Security Directive 26, 'US Policy Toward the Persian Gulf', unclassified text released under the Freedom of Information Act (a facsimile of this document is included in Friedman, *Spider's Web*, pp. 320–2).

Part II:
The Arab World

2

The Gulf War as Arab Civil War

F. GREGORY GAUSE

While the Gulf War was many things, it was also an Arab civil war. It marked the first time that one Arab state militarily invaded and occupied another Arab state.[1] That invasion quickly went beyond the immediate question of Iraq's borders and Kuwait's existence to become a challenge to the domestic legitimacy and stability of the Arab governments that opposed Iraq and joined the American-led coalition against it. Those governments, in turn, questioned the legitimacy of Saddam Hussein's regime and the regimes of those Arab states that sided with Saddam. A full-fledged propaganda war ensued, with efforts by both sides to instigate domestic unrest for their opponents. The inter-Arab atmosphere during this time was reminiscent of the tensions between Arab 'revolutionary' and 'reactionary' regimes in the 1950s and 1960s, when the quest for Arab unity was pursued through cross-border appeals to Arabs in other states to overthrow their governments and clandestine support by Arab governments for domestic factions in other Arab states.[2]

The importance of this 'civil war' element to the politics of the Gulf crisis can be seen from the alliance behavior of the Arab states, including the Palestine Liberation Organization (PLO). That Saudi Arabia and the other Gulf monarchies would align with the United States against Saddam is not hard to understand. Balance-of-power considerations, solidarity with a fellow monarchical regime and fear that at some point Saddam might turn his ambitions against them all pushed them toward Washington. Likewise, Egypt's stand against Iraq was, in social science parlance, 'over-determined'. Balancing against Iraq's regional power (Egypt had taken a similar position when Iraq advanced claims to Kuwait in 1961), Egypt's close ties with the United States and the subsequent Iraqi propaganda campaign against the Egyptian leadership all pointed Egyptian policy in the same direction. However, alliance incentives were much more mixed for other Arab players. Jordan had long relied on the West for security guarantees, and generally had good relations with the Gulf monarchies, yet it sided with Saddam. Syria, ruled like Iraq by the Arab nationalist Ba'th Party and long aligned against the United States, joined the coalition. The PLO had strong financial ties to the Gulf states and had recently made moves to improve its standing in American eyes, but chose the Iraqi side in the crisis. In these cases, the transnational impact of Saddam's invasion on their domestic politics helps to explain their decisions. In Jordan and among Palestinians, public opinion ran strongly in favor of Saddam. To oppose him was politically difficult for both King Hussein and Yasir Arafat. For Syria, a long history of mutual antagonism between the Ba'thist regimes meant that any success for Saddam could lead to increased Iraqi efforts to destabilize the Syrian Ba'th regime both domestically and regionally.

What was striking about the Gulf War episode, however, is how spectacularly unsuccessful these de-legitimation efforts were. Whereas during the 1950s and 1960s a number of Arab governments fell in the face of pressures generated at least in part from abroad, every Arab government weathered the 1990–91 crisis intact. This is remarkable, given the normative barriers that 'Arabism' raised against those regimes (Saudi Arabia, Egypt and Syria) that allied with the United States, Israel's most important international ally, in a war against a fellow Arab state.[3] Equally remarkable was the ability of Saddam Hussein's regime, and those regimes allied with him (Jordan, Yemen and the PLO), to withstand the crushing military defeat of Iraq and the subsequent international and regional pressure upon them. In fact, more than ten years after the Iraqi invasion of Kuwait, not that much has changed in the Arab world. All of the regimes that fought the Gulf War are still in power. Hopes that the experience of the Gulf crisis, with the intense focus of the world media on the region for a protracted period, would spur greater openness in the domestic politics of the Arab states, perhaps even moves toward democracy, have proven empty.

The ability of all the Arab regimes directly involved in this crisis to weather the storms (Desert and other) led some analysts to wonder if the power of transnational identities in the region – Arabism and Islam – to motivate Arabs across state boundaries had irrevocably atrophied. Maybe the Middle East system was on the verge of true 'Westphalianization' – the triumph of *raison d'état* and pure balance-of-power politics over the influence of transnational ideologies that call into question the centrality of purely state identities and loyalties.[4] The progress in the early 1990s in the Arab–Israeli peace process certainly provided evidence of such a trend. However, events of later years in the Middle East indicate that it is too early to pronounce the last rites over the power of transnational identity in the region. Both the Palestinian issue and the suffering of the Iraqi people under economic sanctions have demonstrated a resonance with Arab publics in places that one would not have expected ten years earlier.

This chapter attempts to sort this puzzle out: to account both for the stability of the Arab regimes in the face of enormous pressures during and immediately after the Gulf crisis, and for the continuing power of transnational Arab identity in the politics of the Middle East. It turns first to documenting the intensity of the inter-regime competition during the Gulf crisis, reflected in the efforts by Arab governments to destabilize Arab leaders on the other side of the issue. It then explains the failures of these efforts, by pointing out the extent to which the Arab regimes have strengthened their control over their states and their societies since the 1950s and 1960s. In its final section, it takes up the issue of the enduring power – if much reduced from earlier decades – of transnational identity in the region.

29

INTER-ARAB POLITICS DURING THE GULF CRISIS:
AN ARAB CIVIL WAR

In the first days after his invasion of Kuwait, Saddam Hussein took pains not to threaten Saudi Arabia and its rulers directly. However, once the Saudis accepted the American offer to station troops in the kingdom, Iraq abandoned this restraint and urged the people of Saudi Arabia and the other Gulf monarchies to overthrow their governments. As early as 11 August, Iraqi media outlets called for the overthrow of all 'oil emirs'.[5] By early September these calls had been extended to the rulers of all the Arab states aligned against Iraq, with Saddam saying on 5 September 1990: 'We call upon them [citizens of those Arab states] to revolt against these traitors, their rulers.'[6] An Iraqi source reports that Saddam was confident that this propaganda barrage would destabilize the Saudi domestic scene so thoroughly that Riyadh would have no choice but to reverse its course and accept the new realities.[7] Iraq established clandestine radio stations aimed at Saudi Arabia and Egypt to spread its message,[8] and ratcheted up its invective toward opposing Arab leaders as the crisis wore on. Iraqi attacks on the Saudi leadership were particularly fierce. Playing on the title that Saudi King Fahd had adopted after the Iranian Revolution to emphasize his regime's Islamic credentials, 'Custodian of the Two Holy Mosques' (*khadim al-haramayn al-sharifayn*), Saddam labeled him the 'Traitor of the Two Holy Mosques' (*kha'in al-haramayn al-sharifayn*).[9]

Saddam attempted to play on both Arabist and Islamist sentiments in his mobilization of support in the region. On 12 August 1990 he offered to consider withdrawal from Kuwait if Israel withdrew from occupied Arab lands (and if Syria withdrew from Lebanon), directly linking the Gulf crisis with the Palestinian issue.[10] During the Gulf War, Iraq launched a number of missile attacks on Israel, in an effort to draw Israel into the fighting and thus put greater public opinion pressure on Arab governments supporting the coalition. This Arabist bent was at least consistent with Saddam's own past and the history of the Ba'th Party. More cynical were Saddam's efforts to expropriate

Islamist rhetoric and symbols to support his position. He had himself portrayed as a pious Muslim in the Iraqi media and regularly invoked Quranic passages in his speeches. In January 1991, before the air war began, he ordered the words 'God is great' (Allah al-akbar) to be placed on the Iraqi flag.[11] Given his past history of brutally suppressing Islamist movements within Iraq and of launching a war against the Islamic Republic of Iran, the support that he received from Islamist movements can only be seen as an expression of their greater distaste for the American military presence in the region.[12]

Responses to Saddam's propaganda ploys differed throughout the region. In North Africa, geographically far removed from the crisis, public sentiment seemed to be very pro-Iraqi, though it is hard to gauge with any precision public opinion in any non-democratic country. Despite the fact that Morocco officially supported Saudi Arabia in the crisis, and sent troops to take part in the coalition, public demonstrations supported the Iraqi position.[13] Algerian public opinion, both Arabist and Islamist, united against the coalition war effort.[14] Yemen also witnessed demonstrations in favor of Iraq during the crisis.[15] Given the long history of Saudi–Yemeni tensions, however, those demonstrations were probably motivated as much by anti-Saudi feelings as by pro-Saddam sentiment.

Closer to the locus of the crisis, both Jordanian and Palestinian public opinion were, by all contemporary and subsequent accounts, strongly pro-Iraqi. This is understandable for Palestinians of Islamist, nationalist and Arab nationalist stripes, as Saddam promised to place their cause at the top of the international agenda through his 'linkage' strategy. In Jordan, close economic and political ties with Iraq during the Iran–Iraq War (1980–88) facilitated Iraqi efforts to bolster ties at both the government-to-government and social levels. Combined with the sympathies for Saddam in Jordan's Palestinian community, these ties helped to cement solid public opinion support for Saddam across the political spectrum in Jordan.[16] What is harder to gauge is whether these expressions of public opinion support for Iraq in the crisis drove these governments (including the PLO) to take pro-Iraqi positions, or whether governmental support for Iraq (or, in the North African cases, remove from the heat of the crisis) allowed and encouraged public manifestations of support for Iraq.

In both Egypt and Syria the Iraqi efforts to de-legitimate the governments met with some, though limited, public response. Syrian officials admit that public opinion in their country was generally sympathetic to the Iraqi cause, or at minimum opposed to an American war against an Arab state.[17] There were reports of pro-Saddam protests in Syrian towns shortly after the invasion,[18] and of arrests of students opposed to Syrian participation in the coalition forces.[19] In Egypt, opposition political parties opposed the war against Iraq and a number of protests were held at college campuses.[20] In both countries the authorities suspected Iraq of fomenting domestic opposition. Security services in Egypt believed that Iraq was funding groups planning terrorist actions.[21] The government of Hafiz al-Asad had a long history of bitter conflict with Saddam Hussein that included mutual efforts to destabilize the other domestically.[22] 'Abd al-Halim Khaddam, then Syria's foreign minister, presented a detailed review of Iraqi–Syrian relations to Ba'th Party cadres during the Gulf crisis, to justify Syria's alignment with the United States. He accused Saddam of support for the enemies of the Asad regime, including the Muslim Brotherhood, which had waged a bloody campaign against the regime in the late 1970s and early 1980s: 'Those who talk now about how an Arab soldier could face another Arab soldier in the Gulf, should remember the amount of blood shed in Syria as a result of the support our friends in Baghdad gave to the Muslim Brotherhood gang.'[23] (The very fact that this highly authoritarian regime felt the need to send a senior figure like Khaddam out to justify the policy to its own supporters is a sign of the disquiet the policy provoked in Syrian public opinion.)

In the Gulf states, closest geographically to the crisis and most like Kuwait in terms of politics and society, Saddam's propaganda did not find even minimal levels of public resonance. There was certainly disquiet in some circles, particularly Islamist circles, in Saudi Arabia about the presence of the American forces. One Muslim scholar on the faculty of the Islamic university in Mecca, Safar al-Hawali, published in Saudi Arabia in 1991 a scathing critique of US policy in the Gulf crisis, implicitly very critical of the Saudi regime also, based on sermons and speeches he had given in Saudi mosques during the crisis.[24] Islamists in the kingdom voiced their criticism of Saudi foreign policy and defense policy in a lengthy petition circulated after the Gulf War had ended.[25] However, during the crisis, the Saudi government and other Gulf governments were able to keep the lid on any public manifestations of opposition to their position.

Those Arab governments targeted by Saddam, through both propaganda and more active efforts at destabilization, answered him in kind during and after the Gulf crisis. Saudi Arabia permitted Iraqi opposition forces to set up a radio station, the 'Voice of Free Iraq', in the kingdom in January 1991.[26] The Saudis, as the crisis progressed, quietly tried to assemble a group of former Iraqi political and military figures to act as a potential government-in-exile.[27] Even more significant, Riyadh began during the crisis to reach out to the Iranian-supported Iraqi Shi'i opposition.[28] During his visit to Tehran in June 1991, Saudi Foreign Minister Prince Saud al-Faysal met publicly with Muhammad Baqir al-Hakim, the head of the Supreme Assembly of the Islamic Revolution in Iraq, the Iranian-supported Shi'i opposition group.[29] (Saudi Arabia had supported Iraq in its war with Iran in part to prevent people like al-Hakim from coming to power in Iraq.) The Saudis were certainly hesitant about openly supporting the Shi'i and Kurdish uprisings in Iraq after the Gulf War, preferring that Saddam be overthrown from within the regime. But their preference was clear: an Iraq without Saddam Hussein as ruler.

Syria also encouraged Iraqi opposition during and after the crisis. A number of dissident Iraqi Ba'thists, as well as Iraqi communists, Kurds and liberals, had already made Damascus their headquarters before the Iraqi invasion of Kuwait, taking advantage of the antipathy between the two Ba'thist regimes. These groups formed a 'Joint Action Committee' during the war, and sought support from Saudi Arabia.[30] Beirut, then under the direct control of the Syrian army, hosted a March 1991 meeting of 23 Iraqi opposition groups aimed at concerting their efforts to remove Saddam's regime.[31] The Asad regime did not hide its preferences for change in Iraq. In a front-page editorial in early February 1991, the official daily *al-Thawra* called on the Iraqi people to turn against Saddam and 'liquidate him in cold blood'.[32] An official Ba'th Party document issued just after the Gulf War said that one of Syria's goals in the conflict was 'to support the Iraqi opposition and the popular uprising in its struggle to end the regime that caused the Iraqi people and the Arab world all these tragedies'.[33]

Saudi Arabia also worked during and after the crisis to destabilize those Arab leaders who sided with Iraq in the crisis. The Saudis had the most leverage against, and devoted the most damaging reactions toward, the newly united Republic of Yemen. Yemen had the misfortune to hold the Arab seat on the United Nations (UN) Security Council during the period of the Gulf crisis, magnifying the importance of its position and the anger of the Saudis in reaction. There was a long history of Saudi efforts to influence the politics of Yemen, through aid to the central government and through the maintenance of client relations with important Yemeni tribes and political figures.[34] Once President Ali Abdallah Salih made it clear that Yemen would oppose the dispatch of American forces to the Gulf, the Saudis activated all their levers of influence to make life difficult for him.

The Saudis encouraged Yemeni tribes and political figures to publicly oppose Salih and express their support for Saudi policy, and the Saudi press publicized these expressions.[35] Salih publicly accused the Saudis of trying to destabilize Yemen even before the crisis began, in an effort to disrupt the May 1990 unification agreement between North Yemen and South Yemen.[36] Even more importantly, in late September 1990 the Saudi government enacted new labor regulations requiring Yemenis working in Saudi Arabia to obtain visas and official sponsors. Previously, Yemenis had been the only nationality exempted from these foreign labor requirements. As a result, a massive number of Yemenis, estimated at between 250,000 to 750,000, returned to their homes from Saudi Arabia during the crisis.[37] The economic and social consequences of this repatriation for Yemen were enormous, in terms of remittance income lost, increased unemployment and the social dislocations involved in absorbing that many people.

The Saudis used their economic power to punish the Jordanian and Palestinian leaderships as well. Saudi Arabia halted oil sales at concessionary prices to Jordan, stopped the Jordanian transit trade to the Gulf and cut direct aid to the Jordanian government.[38] Yasir Arafat admitted during the crisis that aid to the PLO from all the Gulf states had been cut off.[39] After the war, Prince Saud al-Faysal met in Damascus with Palestinian leaders opposed to Arafat, and the Middle East rumor mill was full of talk that Riyadh wanted to sponsor an alternative Palestinian leadership.[40]

The 'civil war' aspect of the Gulf crisis in the Arab world is clear. For both sides in the conflict, the issue quickly escalated beyond the Iraqi annexation of Kuwait to become a challenge to the domestic stability and legitimacy of the Arab regimes themselves. But none of the efforts at de-legitimation and de-stabilization succeeded in bringing down Arab regimes, or even in forcing a policy change on any of the Arab regimes. The reason that these tactics, so successfully used by Arab leaders in the 1950s and 1960s, were so unsuccessful in 1990–91 had much to do with changes in the nature of the Arab states.

THE STRENGTHENING OF THE ARAB STATE

The biggest change in the Arab world from the 1950s through the 1990s was the strengthening of the Arab states in relation to Arab societies. In this context 'strength' does not mean military power relative to neighbors and potential foreign threats, but the ability to manage and control domestic society.[41] In an immediate and practical sense, the Arab states of the 1990s have acquired more carrots, with which to vest social interests in the state rather than its competitors, and more sticks, with which to confront domestic enemies. In some states those carrots first came from nationalization of foreign and domestic private sector businesses in the 1950s and 1960s. Since the 1970s, the carrots more often have come from outside the local Arab economies – from oil and gas revenues, from foreign aid – making them uncertain foundations on which to build a state. But the vast increases in oil prices after 1973 have provided Arab oil states with revenues that are of orders of magnitude greater than what they had previously, even with the vagaries of the oil markets in the 1980s and 1990s. Non-oil Arab states also benefited from the revenue inflow, in the form of aid from the oil states and job opportunities for their citizens in the oil economies.

Table 1 indicates how government expenditure as a percentage of gross domestic product(GDP) in a number of Arab states climbed from the 1950s through the early 1980s. Those percentages began to fall in the later 1980s for a number of reasons: lower oil prices, decline in Soviet aid to Syria, tentative moves in Egypt and Jordan toward neo-liberal economic policies. But the expansion of state control over the economy, and thus over society, had been solidified by 20 years of government growth. As the number of carrots has decreased, the role of the sticks in maintaining state control has risen. The conclusion to this chapter will return to the possible implications of a long-term decline of Arab states' control over their economies. For the purposes of explaining behavior in the 1990–91 Gulf crisis, however, it is the growth of the state over the previous two decades that is the key.

The increase in government revenues allowed the Arab states to extend their reach into their societies to an extent unimaginable in the 1950s. Arab state bureaucracies grew enormously, at first in response to the nationalizations of the 1960s (particularly in Egypt) and then to the influx of oil revenues.[42] At a minimum these expanding bureaucracies allowed states to employ more of their citizens, making them directly dependent upon the state. These bureaucracies also increased the capacity of the Arab states to keep watch on and control their societies. That control was certainly not complete, and in many ways was more negative than positive. Arab states could gather the levers of economic and political power into their hands, smother and co-opt civil society and thus prevent things from happening, most notably any successful societal-based efforts to overthrow the ruling regimes. But they were less able to reconstruct their

36

Table 1:
Government Expenditure as a Percentage of GDP

Year	Iraq**	Syria	Jordan	Egypt	Saudi Arabia*
1953	19.2				
1954	19.8			31.0	
1955	21.8			32.3	
1956	26.2				
1957	30.3	12.6⁺			
1958	26.8				
1959			31.4	37.2	
1960	26.9	18.1⁺	33.4	50.9	
1961	28.5		27.5	53.4	
1962	26.9		31.6	64.1	
1963	28.8	26.2	30.5	64.0	31.0
1964	30.6		29.3	62.7	33.4
1965	27.1		28.0	54.5	38.1
1966	27.8	29.8		49.8	42.1
1967	27.6	26.9	41.6		37.6
1968	27.1	30.6	41.4	69.8	37.8
1969			39.4		37.3
1970	30.5		38.0	60.3	36.9
1971	34.5		37.8	59.8	35.5
1972	32.9	28.8	26.3		35.9
1973	43.0	33.6	42.5	71.1	45.9
1974	44.3	34.9	46.0	81.8	32.3
1975		46.9	48.4	59.6	59.9
1976		48.8	47.6	60.1	78.0
1977	66.4	49.4	49.3	47.6	67.3
1978	66.4	41.2	44.3	42.4	65.6
1979		39.2	52.0	44.8	57.6
1980		48.2	44.5		48.2
1981		38.6	40.4	46.0	50.7
1982		49.2	39.3	55.9	53.5
1983		50.8	38.5	43.2	61.6
1984		54.8	36.3	42.3	61.6
1985			36.2	40.1	58.6
1986		34.5	36.4	41.2	50.7
1987		27.8	38.2	35.1	63.0
1988		22.6	41.1	36.6	47.3
1989		25.4	40.7	31.1	48.1
1990		21.8	38.3	27.8	57.9***

Notes:
* From 1963 through 1969, the figure is Saudi government revenue as a percentage of GDP. From 1970 on, the figure is Saudi government expenditure.
** Iraq ceased reporting government financial statistics in the mid-1970s.
*** 1990 figure for Saudi Arabia is combined 1990 and 1991 government spending as a percentage of combined 1990 and 1991 GDP. Because of the Gulf War, Saudi government reported its government budget on a two-year basis for that period.
⁺ Figure refers to GNP.
Sources: See Appendix to this chapter.

Table 2:
Armed Forces per 1,000 of Total Population

Year	Iraq	Syria	Jordan	Egypt	Saudi Arabia
1955	6.7	6.4	16.4	3.5	
1967	9.9	10.8	26.7	5.8	11.5
1977	15.9	29.4	31.8	8.9	13.0
1987	62.9	36.2	29.1	8.6	10.7

Sources: See Appendix to this chapter.

societies along the lines of government dictates. The failure of many ambitious Arab social experiments, like land reform and building efficient state-run industrial sectors, testifies to the limits of Arab governments' powers.[43]

What larger bureaucracies did give state leaders was more instruments for social control than they had previously. One particular part of the burgeoning state bureaucracy in the Arab world, the military and the secret police, gave Arab leaders more and better sticks with which to deter domestic political opposition and suppress it when it arose. Arab states' increasing ability to mobilize manpower into the armed forces over the decades from the 1950s through the 1980s, shown in Table 2, is one indicator of how state capacity translated into increased social control.

The Arab states were able to use their greater resources to provide an increasing level of services to their populations. Aside from jobs in the government bureaucracy, Arab regimes over the past decades have also been able to subsidize basic foodstuffs and public services (electricity, water, telephones, etc.), expand the scope and reach of public education and provide medical care to their people. The extent to which they have been able to provide these goods and services differs according to their circumstances, with the oil-rich states of the Gulf ranking far ahead of the non-oil states. As some Arab states have faced fiscal crises, they have had to scale back the extent to which they subsidize goods and provide services. However, in all the Arab states the governments have used their increased

Table 3:
Percentage of Primary and Secondary School-Age Children in School System

Year	Iraq	Syria	Jordan	Egypt	Saudi Arabia
1950	18	35	27	25	2
1955	24	36	51	36	4
1960	47	44	54	43	7
1965	55	57	69	53	15
1970	49	61	55	49	31
1975	67	71		56	42
1980	89	75	91	62	47
1985	80	87		74	54
1990		84	92*	85	60

Note: * 1989 figure.

Sources: See Appendix to this chapter.

resources and administrative capacity over time to link the material well-being of their citizens directly to the state.

Table 3 demonstrates the vast increase in the states' ability to provide one important service – basic educational opportunities – to their citizens from the 1950s to 1990. What is less clear is the extent to which educating more children in the states' curriculum has increased citizen loyalty to the state itself. Clearly that kind of connection between state education and loyalty has not worked at the regime level. There have been enough instances of popular discontent with Arab leaders to put paid to the notion that going to a state school makes you 'love the leader'. But it is at least a plausible hypothesis to connect the decline in the salience of transnational ideological attachments in the Middle East to the increasing number of students who have been through state schools. Exposure from their earliest days to government-written curricula that present the state as the first and most important locus of political identity and loyalty, as the basis of their larger Arab and Muslim identities, has undoubtedly affected their political outlooks (though to what extent is difficult to measure in these authoritarian regimes). This increase in educational opportunities can also be seen as another example of the extension of state control throughout society. A new school in a rural area is frequently the first regular presence of 'the state' in the countryside, and the local teacher the first permanent state employee there. The school can be the base from which other state services and state instruments of control connect to the local community.

This growing state capacity, and the increased relevance of the state in the everyday lives of citizens that it brings, has many negative consequences: stifling bureaucratic controls on individual initiative in the economy, a dulling conformity in the official media, oppressive security apparatuses. But the relevance of the state concentrates political activity, be it supportive or oppositional, into the arena of the existing state entities rather than allowing it to search for some hypothetical alternative form of political organization. Transnational agendas address less and less the immediate political problems that people face, and those who are attracted to such agendas face much more powerful state opponents. Increased state capacity is certainly not a foolproof guarantee of regime stability. The success of Iran's Islamic revolution proves that. The increasing role of the state can politicize people in opposition to regimes, as Islamic movements throughout the Arab world demonstrate. However, stronger Arab states make their regimes better able to meet opposition challenges. They particularly increase the ability of Arab regimes to counter efforts to destabilize them from abroad, through a mix of propaganda, pressure and subversion, as Saddam Hussein attempted with his Arab enemies and his Arab enemies attempted in return with him (and his Arab allies).

THE CONTINUING RELEVANCE OF TRANSNATIONAL IDENTITY IN THE ARAB WORLD

The strengthening of the Arab state over the past five decades provides the best explanation for the remarkable stability of the Arab regimes during the Gulf crisis and after, in comparison to the endemic instability of Arab regimes during regional crises in the 1950s and 1960s. The salience of transnational ideological platforms like pan-Arabism and Islamist political appeals, at least as challengers to existing states and regimes, is much reduced from that earlier period. However, it would be a mistake to conclude from this that these transnational identities have lost all their relevance in the politics of the Middle East. Events at the end of the 1990s and the beginning of the 2000s, particularly regarding the Palestinian and Iraqi issues, show that Arab populations can still be mobilized to support their fellow Arabs across borders. The important question is in what circumstances, and to what extent, are these transnational identities relevant for Arab regimes and Arab foreign policy stances.

The Iraqi issue, as it played out at the end of the 1990s and the beginning of the 2000s, highlights the continuing role that pan-Arab sympathies play in the foreign policies of Arab states. It is not surprising that states aligned with Iraq in the Gulf War would oppose the international sanctions regime on Baghdad. They presumably sided with Saddam because they saw some strategic and/or economic benefit for themselves in a strong Iraq. One might even be able to account for Egypt's stance against the sanctions on balance-of-power grounds. Iraq remains physically removed from Egypt, and thus not as immediate a threat. A weakened Iraq means that Iran can play a larger role in Gulf politics, something that Cairo would also see as problematic. However, it is hard to see how, on pure balance-of-power grounds, either Syria or the Gulf states would want to see any strengthening of Saddam Hussein. Yet these states, even Kuwait,[44] have also come out publicly against continued economic sanctions on Iraq, and have been increasingly vocal (with the exception of Kuwait) in their condemnation of American military strikes against Iraq.

Syria has not only called for lifting economic sanctions on Iraq, but in 2000 began to buy oil from Iraq, shipped by pipeline (a pipeline closed by Syria in 1982, when Iraq was at war with Iran) to Syria, in return for which Syria has been paying Iraq directly, outside of the United Nations' 'oil for food' program that requires buyers of Iraqi oil to pay into a UN escrow account.[45] Syrian airplanes also participated in the crumbling of the air boycott against Iraq in the latter months of 2000, when civilian airliners from a number of Arab and non-Arab countries began to fly to Baghdad. Syrian officials regularly condemned

41

American and British air attacks on Iraq, including the attack of February 2001 that perhaps signaled that the Bush administration would take a militarily tougher line against Saddam Hussein.[46]

The Gulf states, with perhaps the most to fear from a revived Iraq under Saddam's control, have also begun to distance themselves from American policy toward Iraq. Saudi Arabia openly criticized the air attacks on Iraq in February 2001.[47] Even Kuwait, as mentioned above, has begun to call for a revision of the economic sanctions regime. Those kinds of calls, emphasizing the costs of sanctions for the Iraqi people, have been coming from the leaders of the United Arab Emirates (UAE) for years.[48] At least in part, these moves toward a more accommodating policy toward Iraq emanate from increased public perceptions that the Iraqi sanctions do nothing to the regime, but place an intolerable burden on the Iraqi people. This theme is frequently raised in the semi-official press and in meetings that Gulf officials and intellectuals have with visiting Westerners.

The other issue on which pan-Arab sentiment continues to animate people across state lines in the Arab world is the Palestinian issue. That is not a surprising fact in Jordan, where over half the population is of Palestinian descent, or perhaps even in Egypt, with a long history of involvement in the Palestinian issue, despite the formal peace treaties each of those countries has with Israel. But even in the Gulf states, furthest removed geographically from the Arab–Israeli arena, where Yasir Arafat's alignment with Saddam Hussein during the Gulf War is still bitterly remembered, sympathy for the Palestinians remains high. With the collapse of the peace process in late 2000 and the renewal of Israeli–Palestinian violence, Gulf voices were raised not only against Israel, but against the United States as well.[49] Public calls for boycotts of American products, in solidarity with the Palestinians, found some popular response in the Gulf states.[50] The two Gulf states that had opened formal trade relations with Israel, Qatar and Oman, both closed the Israeli trade offices in their capitals in the fall of 2000, in response to the renewed violence.[51] Saudi Arabia's Crown Prince Abdallah turned down an invitation from the Bush administration to visit the White House, extended in May 2001, according to press reports because of his dissatisfaction with American inaction on the Arab–Israeli peace process.[52]

The Iraqi and Palestinian issues, as they have developed at the end of the 1990s and the outset of the 2000s, show how transnational feelings of Arab identification can still constrain the choices that Arab leaders have in their foreign policies. In both cases there is popular sympathy for the plight of fellow Arabs. In neither case is that popular sympathy immediately threatening to the Arab regimes themselves. Arab publics which are sympathetic towards Iraqis and Palestinians are not automatically expressing displeasure with their own rulers, as might have been the case if they expressed that sympathy in Saudi Arabia during the Gulf War. Neither Yasir Arafat nor Saddam Hussein present any *immediate* threat to the stability of the Saudi, Jordanian or Egyptian regimes. Therefore, there is no immediate cost to Arab regimes in allowing that sympathy to be expressed in the public sphere, or even in a limited way allowing that public sympathy to affect foreign policy. This is seen, in fact, as a useful way to deflect popular discontent that might be present against the regimes themselves. The personal feelings of Arab leaders, of sympathy for and solidarity with Palestinians and the Iraqi public, should not be discounted either.

However, none of the Arab regimes are willing to allow that public sympathy for Iraqis and Palestinians to push them into foreign policy decisions that might affect their immediate interests. Egypt and Jordan are not abrogating their peace treaties with Israel. The Gulf states are not embargoing oil to the West or cutting their defense ties with the United States. There are limits to which the regimes will allow these real public sentiments to affect their decisions. Pan-Arab sympathies still exist, and governments react to them and manage them, even taking them into account in ways that do not affect immediate regime security interests. No regime can afford to be seen as ignoring those sympathies. But that is much different from earlier periods in modern Arab history, when Arab regimes were made and unmade by such transnational movements. The change might be somewhat the result of the declining appeal of those transnational ideological appeals to Arab publics, but it is more the result of the strengthening of the Arab state itself.

CONCLUSION

Indications are that the two overall trends identified above: the strengthening of the Arab state, in terms of its control over Arab societies; and the continuing – if reduced – relevance of transnational identities of pan-Arabism and Islam among Arab publics, will continue in the future. Arab regimes will most probably have the means to manage the public opinion pressures that arise in the foreign policy sphere from these transnational identities, but they will not be able to ignore them. Their foreign policies will reflect state and regime interests on bedrock issues of security, but when their security is not directly at risk they will be tempted to score points with public opinion (and perhaps reflect the leaders' own personal sympathies) by tacking with the pan-Arab and Islamist winds.

Two factors have arisen which could challenge the status quo forecast set out in the previous paragraph. The first is the decline, which began in the late 1980s, of the level of control Arab states are exercising over their economies, at least as measured in the percentage of GDP accounted for by government spending (see Table 1). The trends of political democratization and economic liberalization that dominated most parts of the developing world in the 1980s and 1990s largely passed the Arab states by. None have privatized economically to the extent that many Latin American and East Asian countries have, or even to the extent that Middle Eastern neighbors Turkey and Israel have. Their resistance to such moves stems from their unwillingness to give up the power and control that the state-led economic model gives them, and their fear of the political ramifications of the short-term economic costs that neo-liberal transitions place upon middle and lower-middle class citizens (reduced or lifted subsidies, higher prices, increased unemployment).

However, under the press of relatively lower oil prices, the crises of state-led growth models, pressure from leading powers and economic institutions and the sheer momentum of neo-liberal ideas, Arab governments are beginning to take steps toward limiting the role of the state in the economy. Some Arab states are further along this road than others. Tunisia and Morocco have led the way; Egypt and Jordan have begun to take significant steps; Saudi Arabia and other oil producers are talking the talk, but just beginning to walk the walk; Syria brings up the rear. These steps have taken place under the continuing dominance of the state as regulator of the economy and ultimate controller of the banking and financial systems. Like the Chinese communist rulers, Arab leaders are hoping to get the benefits of more marketized economies without giving up their ultimate political control over economy and society.

To the extent that the 'Chinese model' proves successful, Arab state control over Arab society will continue unabated, even as the percentage share of GDP accounted for by government spending declines. On the other hand, if the more optimistic proponents of 'globalization' are correct, continued marketization of Arab economies will mean more personal autonomy for Arab citizens, independent civil societies and freer political systems. It is doubtful that such a profound socio-economic change could occur without profound political instability and regime change. If economic trends in the Arab world do bring about greater political freedoms, it is possible that the power of transnational identities in the Arab world will increase. At a minimum, governments will not be able to control the political energies of their citizens to the extent that they do now, and therefore might feel even more compelled than they do now to orient their foreign policies toward Arab nationalist and Islamist causes. The jury remains out on what the ultimate political effects of more liberal economic policies in the Arab world will be.

The second factor that could increase the political power of transnational identities in the Arab world is the growing phenomenon of all-Arab media outlets, particularly satellite television.[53] Most of these new media outlets are connected to specific Arab governments (for example, al-Jazeera satellite television, the most popular Arabic-language news station, owned by the Qatari ruling family), but they perforce must appeal to audiences larger than the citizens of their own state. Targeting an all-Arab audience across state lines, they inevitably play to and reinforce common Arab cultural identity. Islamist movements have not gotten into the transnational media game at the same level of technological sophistication, but that seems to be more a matter of time than any insuperable ideological or technological barrier. On the news side, these new media outlets emphasize issues, like the Palestinian struggle against Israel and the plight of Iraqis under sanctions, that cut across Arab state lines. This is a new phenomenon in the Arab world, and social commentators are extremely hesitant to pronounce on its political effects. Within these cautious parameters, however, some analysts do see the new media as a potential building-block for a resurgence of pan-Arab identity.[54]

As with the trends in government control over the economy, the ultimate political effects of the new media in the Arab world remain to be seen. But the new media represent one of the few avenues, amidst the state-controlled local media and school systems, for pan-Arab and pan-Islamist messages not vetted and approved by Arab governments to reach large numbers of Arab citizens. If these transnational identities stage a 'comeback' in the new millennium, the new Arab media will undoubtedly be one of the major reasons. Until there is more evidence of their power to mobilize Arabs on these platforms, however, the safer bet is to assume that the patterns in Arab state foreign policy behavior seen during the Gulf crisis of 1990–91 will continue to operate in the future.

APPENDIX: SOURCES FOR TABLES

Table 1

Iraq: Government expenditures 1953–68 taken from Central Bank of Iraq, *Bulletin*, 4 (October–December 1970); Government expenditures 1970–74 taken from Central Statistical Organization, Ministry of Planning, Republic of Iraq,

Annual Abstract of Statistics 1976, Table 10/2; GDP figures for 1953–54 and 1956–58 taken from K. Haseeb, *The National Income of Iraq, 1953–1961* (London: Oxford University Press, 1964), Table 6; GDP figures for 1955 and 1959–74 taken from International Monetary Fund (IMF), *International Financial Statistics Yearbook*, 1987; The 1977 and 1978 estimates are taken from Economist Intelligence Unit (EIU), *Quarterly Economic Review of Iraq – Annual Supplement, 1979* (London: EIU, 1979).

Syria: Government expenditures 1956–68 taken from Central Bureau of Statistics, Syrian Arab Republic, *Statistical Abstract 1969–70* (Damascus: Government Printing Press, 1971), Table 153; Government expenditures 1972–75 taken from IMF, *Syrian Arab Republic – Recent Economic Documents*, SM/77/139, 17 June 1977, Table 14; Government expenditures 1976–84 taken from IMF, *Government Finance Statistics Yearbook*, 1986; Government expenditures 1986–90 taken from IMF, *International Financial Statistics Yearbook*, 1994; gross national product (GNP) for 1957 and 1960 taken from Bureau de Documentations Syriennes et Arabes, *Syrie 1964* (Damascus); GDP for 1963 taken from Central Bureau of Statistics, Syrian Arab Republic, *Statistical Abstract 1969–70* (Damascus: Government Printing Press, 1971), Table 261; GDP for 1964–84, 1986–90 taken from IMF, *International Financial Statistics Yearbook*, various years.

Jordan: Government expenditures 1959 taken from Department of Statistics, Hashemite Kingdom of Jordan, *Statistical Yearbook 1964* (Amman: Department of Statistics Press, n.d.), Table 103; Government expenditures 1960–65 taken from Central Bank of Jordan, *Quarterly Bulletin*, 2, 3 (1966); Government expenditures 1967–90 taken from IMF, *International Financial Statistics Yearbook*, 1994; GDP for 1959–65, 1967–90 taken from IMF, *International Financial Statistics Yearbook*, various years.

Egypt: Government expenditures 1954–66 taken from National Bank of Egypt, *Economic Bulletin*, 24, 1 (1971), Table 2/1; Government expenditures 1968 taken from National Bank of

Egypt, *Economic Bulletin*, 21, 4 (1968), Table IV; Government expenditures 1970–71 taken from National Bank of Egypt, *Economic Bulletin*, 24, 3 (1971), Tables II, III; Government expenditures 1973-74 taken from National Bank of Egypt, *Economic Bulletin*, 28, 1 (1974); Government expenditures 1975 through 1990 taken from IMF, *International Financial Statistics Yearbook*, 1998; GDP for 1954 taken from National Bank of Egypt, *Economic Bulletin*, 24, 2 (1971), Table 7/1; GDP for 1955–74 taken from IMF, *International Financial Statistics Yearbook*, 1987; GDP for 1975–90 taken from IMF, *International Financial Statistics Yearbook*, 1998.

Saudi Arabia: Government revenue figures 1963–69 taken from Nadav Safran, *Saudi Arabia: Ceaseless Quest for Security* (Cambridge, MA: Harvard University Press, 1985), pp. 108, 183; Government expenditures 1970–90 taken from Saudi Arabian Monetary Agency (SAMA), *Annual Report*, 2000 (available at www.sama.gov.sa/english/statistical/annual); GDP figures taken from IMF, *International Financial Statistics Yearbook*, various years.

Table 2

1955 population and armed forces figures taken from J.C. Hurewitz, *Middle East Politics: The Military Dimension* (Boulder, CO: Westview Press, 1982); Figures for 1967, 1977 and 1987 taken from International Institute for Strategic Studies, *Military Balance*, 1967/68, 1977/78 and 1987/88 editions, with the following exceptions: Jordanian population figure for 1977 taken from Hashemite Kingdom of Jordan, *Statistical Yearbook 1977*. In each case the *Military Balance* population figure was widely discrepant with other sources and with other annual issues of the same source. Party militias, paramilitary forces, gendarmes, etc. were not included in the armed forces numbers because statistics on these forces are less reliable.

Table 3

United Nations Educational, Scientific and Cultural Organization (UNESCO), *Statistical Yearbook*, various years.

NOTES

1. The Gulf War was certainly not the first time one Arab state had sent forces into another Arab state. On a number of occasions Arab governments have invited the forces of other Arab governments into their territories, be it to confront Israel, to balance threats from Arab neighbors (as Kuwait did in 1961, when it invited Egyptian and Saudi forces to its territory to check Iraqi claims against it) or to confront domestic enemies (for example, Egyptian forces in North Yemen during the civil war in the 1960s). Syrian forces were formally invited into Lebanon by the Lebanese government in 1975, and their presence in Lebanon given an Arab League imprimatur in 1976, though the autonomy of the Lebanese government at that time can be called into question. There have been numerous border skirmishes between Arab states, and bloody confrontations between Arab state forces and Palestinian militias. The most blatant example of inter-Arab military confrontation before 1990 was the Syrian invasion of Jordan in 1970, in support of the Palestinian forces during the Jordanian civil war.

2. See Patrick Seale, *The Struggle for Syria* (New Haven, CT: Yale University Press, 1986); and Malcolm Kerr, *The Arab Cold War* (New York: Oxford University Press, 1970).

3. The centrality of not aligning with Western powers to the normative meaning of 'Arabism' is stressed by Michael Barnett, *Dialogues in Arab Politics: Negotiations in Regional Order* (New York: Columbia University Press, 1998).

4. Barnett entitled his penultimate chapter 'The End of the Arab States System?'. See also the analysis about changes in Arab thinking about the regional system in Ibrahim Karawan, 'Arab Dilemmas in the 1990s: Breaking Taboos and Searching for Signposts', *Middle East Journal*, 48, 3 (Summer 1994).

5. *New York Times*, 12 August 1990, section 4, p. 1.

6. *New York Times*, 6 September 1990, p. A19.

7. Sa'd al-Bazzaz, *al-ganaralat akhir man ya'lam* [The Generals are the Last to Know] (Amman: al-Ahliyya Publishing and Distribution, 1996), p. 112.

8. *New York Times*, 16 September 1990, section 4, p. 3.

9. *New York Times*, 31 December 1990, p. 6.

10. See text of his 'linkage' proposal in Ofra Bengio (ed.), *Saddam Speaks on the Gulf Crisis: A Collection of Documents* (Tel Aviv: Moshe Dayan Center for Middle Eastern and African Studies, Tel Aviv University, 1992), pp. 124–6.

11. *New York Times*, 14 January 1991, p. 1.

12. On Islamist movements' reactions to the Gulf War, see James Piscatori (ed.), *Islamic Fundamentalisms and the Gulf Crisis* (Chicago, IL: Fundamentalism Project, American Academy of Arts and Sciences, 1991). An example of this tension in the position of Islamist movements toward the Gulf crisis can be found in the press release issued by a number of prominent Islamist activists (including Rashid al-Ghanushi of Tunisia, Hassan al-Turabi of Sudan, Necmettin Erbakan of Turkey) in December 1990, following a mediation effort that took them to Saudi Arabia, Iraq and Iran. The group expressed support for 'guaranteeing the freedom of the Kuwaiti people in their homeland' and called for an 'Arab–Islamic solution' that would lead to Iraqi withdrawal from Kuwait, but stressed their 'revulsion over the presence of foreign forces in the Arabian Peninsula and the Gulf, and the threat their continued

presence poses to the security of the region, its holy places, its traditions and its natural resources'. The press release can be found in the Islamist journal *al-Insan*, 3 (December 1990).

13. *New York Times*, 4 February 1991, p. 9.
14. Hugh Roberts, 'A Trial of Strength: Algerian Fundamentalism', in Piscatori, *Islamic Fundamentalisms and the Gulf Crisis*, pp. 131–54.
15. *New York Times*, 11 August 1990, p. 1; 12 August 1990, p. 12.
16. In over 20 interviews with Jordanian officials, academics and observers conducted in May 1991, the author found the unanimous view that Jordanian public opinion was uniformly pro-Saddam during the Gulf crisis, and that this fact seriously constrained King Hussein's freedom of maneuver in the diplomacy of the crisis. This conclusion is supported by others who have done field work in Jordan on this question: Laurie Brand, *Jordan's Inter-Arab Relations: The Political Economy of Alliance Decision-Making* (New York: Columbia University Press, 1994), pp. 284–95; Marc Lynch, *State Interests and Public Spheres: The International Politics of Jordan's Identity* (New York: Columbia University Press, 1999), Chap. 5.
17. Author interviews with current and former Syrian government officials in Damascus, March 1998.
18. *New York Times*, 30 August 1990, p. 16.
19. *New York Times*, 17 February 1991, p. 21.
20. *New York Times*, 25 January 1991, p. 11; 27 February 1991, p. 22.
21. *New York Times*, 11 November 1990, p. 14.
22. For the background on this intra-Ba'thist conflict, see Eberhard Kienle, *Ba'th vs. Ba'th: The Conflict between Syria and Iraq, 1968–1989* (London: I.B. Taurus, 1990). Hafiz al-Asad's biographer, Patrick Seale, wrote: 'Incestuously involved with one another, the Iraqi and Syrian Ba'th parties were riven by mutual distrust as each was convinced that the other had planted a Trojan horse in its ranks.' Patrick Seale, *Asad: The Struggle for the Middle East* (Berkeley, CA: University of California Press, 1988), p. 354.
23. See Khaddam statement reproduced in Ahmad Ajaj, 'As'ad 'Ubur and Sa'd al-Qasim, *al-I'lam al-Suri wa Azmat al-Khalij* [The Syrian Media and the Gulf Crisis] (Damascus: al-Thawra Newspaper, 1992), pp. 297–8.
24. Safar ibn 'Abd al-Rahman al-Hawali, *Haqa'iq Hawl Azmat al-Khalij* [Truths about the Gulf Crisis] (Mecca: Dar Mecca al-Mukarrama, 1991). For a discussion of al-Hawali and other Saudi Islamists, see Mamoun Fandy, *Saudi Arabia and the Politics of Dissent* (New York: St Martin's Press, 1999).
25. F. Gregory Gause, III, *Oil Monarchies: Domestic and Security Challenges in the Arab Gulf States* (New York: Council on Foreign Relations Press, 1994), pp. 35–7.
26. *New York Times*, 16 April 1991, p. 9.
27. *New York Times*, 22 February 1991, p. 8.
28. The Saudi media signaled this switch by beginning to feature news on Iraqi Shi'i organizations. For example, see the following interviews and articles: interview with Muhammad Taqi Mudarrasi, spokesman for the Islamic Action Organization in Iraq, in *al-Sharq al-Awsat*, 13 March 1991, p. 5; interview with Muwaffiq al-Rubay', a member of the politburo of al-Da'wa party, the oldest Shi'i Islamic opposition group in Iraq, ibid., 6 March 1991, p. 5; interview with Hussein al-Sadr, nephew of Ayatallah Muhammad Baqir al-Sadr, who was killed by the Iraqi government in 1980, ibid., 11 February 1991, p. 6; and a flattering article on Muhammad Baqir al-Hakim, the leader of the Iranian-sponsored Supreme Assembly of the Islamic Revolution in Iraq, ibid., 5 March 1991, p. 5.
29. *al-Hayat*, 7 June 1991, pp. 1, 7.
30. *New York Times*, 22 February 1991, p. 8.
31. *al-Hayat*, 14 March 1991, pp. 1, 7.
32. Cited in *New York Times*, 10 February 1991, p. 18.
33. Hizb al-Ba'th al-'Arabi al-Ishtiraki, al-Qiyada al-Qawmiyya, Maktab al-Imana

al-'Amma [Arab Ba'th Socialist Party, National Command, Office of the Secretariat General], *Azmat al-Khalij: al-Muqaddamat wa al-Nata'ij wa Afaq al-Mustaqbal* [The Gulf Crisis: Background, Results and Views of the Future], Political and Economic Studies Series, 41 (Damascus; July 1991).

34. For the background on Saudi–Yemeni relations, see F. Gregory Gause, III, *Saudi–Yemeni Relations: Domestic Structures and Foreign Influence* (New York: Columbia University Press, 1990).

35. See, for example, statements and telegrams from Yemeni tribal sheikhs in *al-Sharq al-Awsat*, 17 August 1990, p. 5; 23 August 1990, p. 4; and 21 September 1990, p. 2. The latter telegram describes Yemeni President Salih as 'an ignorant Sanhani' (one of Yemen's smaller tribes) and his leadership as 'parasitical and without conscience'.

36. Interview with Salih in *New York Times*, 26 October 1990, pp. A1, A11.

37. The figure of 750,000 was cited in the *New York Times*, 28 November 1990, p. A14. An account of the changed Saudi labor regulations can be found in *al-Hayat*, 21 September 1990, p. 1.

38. Author interview, Jordanian Foreign Ministry, May 1991.

39. *New York Times*, 26 November 1990, p. 12.

40. *New York Times*, 8 March 1991, p. 8.

41. This argument is developed at length in F. Gregory Gause, III, 'Sovereignty, Statecraft and Stability in the Middle East', *Journal of International Affairs*, 45, 2 (Winter 1992) and 'Revolutionary Fevers and Regional Contagion: Domestic Structures and the "Export" of Revolution in the Middle East', *Journal of South Asian and Middle Eastern Studies*, 14, 3 (Spring 1991). For an extended discussion of these themes in the cases of Iraq and Syria, see Malik Mufti, *Sovereign Creations: Pan-Arabism and Political Order in Syria and Iraq* (Ithaca, NY: Cornell University Press, 1996). Nazih Ayubi questions whether the Arab states are actually getting stronger, in that they have not developed strong linkages with civil society that would facilitate revenue extraction and popular acceptance of government policy, *Overstating the Arab State: Politics and Society in the Middle East* (London: I.B. Tauris, 1995), particularly Chap. 12. However, he concedes that the Arab states are getting 'harder' and 'fiercer' (pp. 449–50), in that they control more means of coercion, more resources and greater administrative reach than was the case previously. Ayubi's provocative analysis implicitly compares contemporary Arab states to non-Arab contemporary democracies, not to the Arab states as they were in the 1950s.

42. Nazih Ayubi, 'Arab Bureaucracies: Expanding Size, Changing Roles', in Adeed Dawisha and I. William Zartman (eds), *Beyond Coercion: The Durability of the Arab State* (New York: Croom Helm, 1988).

43. See Joel Migdal, *Strong Societies and Weak States* (Princeton, NJ: Princeton University Press, 1988), Chap. 5, on the failures of Nasser's state to completely restructure Egypt's agricultural economy. On the general failure in the state-led industrial sector, see Alan Richards and John Waterbury, *A Political Economy of the Middle East* (Boulder, CO: Westview Press, 1996; 2nd edn), Chaps 7 and 8.

44. In January 2001, the Kuwaiti Foreign Minister, Sheikh Sabah al-Ahmad al-Sabah, publicly praised a Kuwaiti editorial writer for calling for a lifting of economic sanctions on Iraq and a refocus of the sanctions regime on the Iraqi leadership, not the Iraqi people. See *Gulf News* (UAE), 24 January 2001, accessed through Gulf/2000 project website, www1.columbia.edu/sec/cu/sipa/GULF2000.

45. On the Iraqi–Syria oil deal, see *Petroleum Intelligence Weekly*, 5 February 2001, p. 7; *Washington Post*, 18 February 2001, p. A1. US Secretary of State Colin Powell apparently obtained a Syrian commitment in late February 2001 to begin paying into the UN escrow account for its Iraqi oil purchases, though when Syria will begin to abide by the sanctions regime was not clear. *New York Times*, 27 February 2001, p. 1.

46. See *Washington Post*, 27 February 2001, p. 1; *al-Hayat*, 19 February 2001, pp. 1, 6.

47. *Washington Post*, 27 February 2001, p. 1.
48. See, for example, 'UAE President Urges New Page with Iraq', *Reuters*, 16 October 1995.
49. See the review article on Gulf press reaction to US Secretary of State Madeline Albright's visit to the region in October 2000, 'Gulf Arab Papers Blast US During Albright Visit', *Reuters*, 18 October 2000, accessed through Gulf/2000 project website.
50. 'Calls to Boycott US Sweep Gulf', *Associated Press*, 30 November 2000, accessed through Gulf/2000 project website.
51. 'Oman Severs Low-Level Ties with Israel', *Reuters*, 12 October 2000; 'Qatar Closes Israeli Trade Mission', *Associated Press*, 9 November 2000, both accessed through Gulf/2000 project website.
52. *New York Times*, 17 May 2001.
53. For an excellent introduction to the subject, see Jon Alterman, 'The Middle East's Information Revolution', *Current History*, 99, 633 (January 2000), pp. 21–6.
54. For a cautious assessment in this direction, see Edmund Ghareeb, 'New Media and the Information Revolution in the Arab World: An Assessment', *Middle East Journal*, 54, 3 (Summer 2000), pp. 395–418. For a contrary view, which emphasizes the continuing distrust among Arab citizens of state-connected media, see Mamoun Fandy, 'Information Technology, Trust and Social Change in the Arab World', *Middle East Journal*, 54, 3 (Summer 2000), pp. 378–94.

3

The Arab World: Ten Years after the Gulf War

GABRIEL BEN-DOR

The Gulf War of 1990–91 shattered a good many conventions in the Middle East in general and in the Arab world in particular, a momentous event which has left an indelible impression on the political soul of the region. The facts of the case seem simple enough. One large country, Iraq, invaded a smaller one, Kuwait, conquered it within a matter of hours and decided to annex it officially and turn it into a province, thereby taking over the prodigious oil wealth found in the smaller country. In response, the leaders of the world organized a coalition of countries that pressured the aggressors to withdraw, and, when the latter failed to comply, the coalition initiated a war in which the conquered territory was liberated and returned to its rightful owners. The aggressor country has been held in check ever since, as the coalition keeps imposing restrictions on its sovereignty by a variety of means, some of them economic and others military in nature.

Yet, the total situation was not only extremely complicated, but also involved some of the most cherished values of regional politics. For this was a case in which one Arab country invaded another, openly and blatantly, after which the invaded country was liberated by an international coalition of countries, led by those that the Arab world normally holds responsible for its plight.

The entire discourse of this generation of Arab leaders and intellectuals is dominated by the talk about colonialism and imperialism as the primary cause of all the troubles of the Arabs. For these troubles, Americans and British are held primarily responsible. They are the enemy, the devil, symbols of everything that is wrong with the world in general and the Arab world in particular. Yet now, when the chips were down, it was the good old imperialist enemy that came to rescue the Arabs from their own plight. It turned out, to the enormous embarrassment of the Arabs, that they could not settle their own internal problems, and that they needed outside help for resolving the problems that they always held to be uniquely their own.

Indeed, it was exactly for this type of eventuality that the Arabs had built up special regional institutions, such as the Arab League (which they had used, for instance, in the case of Lebanon, to put together a series of resolutions, which then were imposed by the force of an Arab Deterrent Force, which in prac-tice meant the Syrian army in Lebanon). But now this mecha-nism failed totally, for the Iraqi aggressors paid no attention to outside pressures, and their military might was clearly sufficient to repel any external regional military attempt to liberate Kuwait. Thus, acute embarrassment ensued. To do nothing was not possible, although a great many Arab intellectuals and lead-ers were so tempted, for many reasons. Evidently, to do anything useful would be most difficult, so many people wanted to disguise this difficulty by simply ignoring the problem. Also, many people showed indifference to the fate of Kuwait, out of hatred for the corrupt feudal regime of that country. Furthermore, quite a few radicals in the region actually felt that the leader of Iraq, Saddam Hussein, by his extremist rhetoric, represented their cause, and, furthermore, looked up to him for acting in a way that others dared only to speak of.

Alternatively, the price of doing nothing was also very high. After all, the leader of one powerful country had simply swal-lowed another, lock, stock and barrel. Given that many Arab countries had no natural boundaries, and they themselves were artificial creatures carved out by the European imperialists for their own nebulous purposes, to do nothing would be an extremely dangerous precedent. This way of conquest simply could not be accepted.

A large number of countries, rich in oil resources, were at the same time small either in territory, or in population, or both.

These countries would not be able to withstand the assault of the larger countries that often cast greedy eyes on their riches. Among these countries one should mention Saudi Arabia, Qatar, Oman, Bahrain, the UAE and, in particular, Abu Dhabi and Dubai. Clearly, once the principle of acquiring other countries by force was accepted, there was no telling where this would stop. And to the list of the countries endangered one had to add several others, such as Lebanon, Jordan, Libya and perhaps even others. In short, many Arab countries would be in danger of being devoured by one or more of the strong military powers in the Arab world (among them Egypt, Iraq and Syria) if the Iraqi conquest of Kuwait were not cancelled.

In fact, in the past there had been inter-Arab invasions, practically all of them failures, among them the Egyptian attempt to dominate Yemen by force of arms; the Syrian attempt to invade Jordan in 1970; the possible Egyptian attempts to invade Libya. The single case of Lebanon stands in contrast to the above as it officially invited the outside forces in. This invitation was in consequence of its inability to resolve the internal problems of the country on its own. Furthermore, the presence of the outside forces was legitimized in official resolutions of the Arab League, accepted unanimously in the meetings of that forum. Also, the country was not officially annexed to the invading one. In any event, Lebanon is unique in terms of its population and political structure. Thus, Lebanon is not in a comparable category with Kuwait. Crucially, no evidence exists that the case of Lebanon touched the Arab political soul in any profound way, whereas the case of Kuwait is entirely different.

Indeed, the invasion might have turned out entirely differently had it taken place under different circumstances: had it been launched earlier, when the world was still bipolar; had it been launched later, when the Iraqi program of building weapons of mass destruction had advanced much further. But as it turned out, a relatively fortunate combination of circumstances occurred: the unipolar nature of the international system allowed a strong response on the part of the international community; and the Iraqi program for the development of mass destruction capabilities, while frightening enough to provoke a sense of fear around the region, was not sufficient to deter the others from acting.

Survival was the challenge, and the most important impera-tive of the regimes around the region. They could live with all kinds of regional and ideological anomalies, but they could not live with the precedent of countries being swallowed up by their neighbors. They had to make sure that this precedent would not survive the test of regional and international reaction as other-wise their own future would be in grave jeopardy.

After the Iraqi invasion, Iraq showed no inclination to give in to international diplomatic pressure, and seemingly nothing short of military action would be sufficient to force it out of Kuwait. The Arab world had to face the necessity of forcing Iraq out of Kuwait, an acutely embarrassing situation. After all, the Arab League could not even adopt the appropriate resolutions to allow military action, for the *modus operandi* of the League is more or less based on the principle of unanimity: countries that do not vote for the League's resolutions are not bound by them, even formally. Clearly, Iraqi voting against the resolution would be enough to make it fail on the official level.

Crucially, Arab military force was simply inadequate to face the Iraqis, who had almost a million men under arms, organized in 65 divisions, with a large air force, and with naval capabilities far exceeding those of the other countries. Furthermore, grave logistical problems existed in moving Arab forces from across the region to face the Iraqi invading army. In short, such a military response did not appear practical. As a consequence, the Arabs had to make a truly embarrassing choice. They could accept the Iraqi conquest of Kuwait, unchangeable by any means other than force, or else they could rely on the force of others to expel Iraq. After a short period of a rather difficult hesitation, they chose the latter course, and therein lies a lesson.

Joining the erstwhile forces of colonialism and imperialism was a step almost unimaginable for an entire generation of Arabs. Nothing worse could be imagined, really, than voluntari-ly teaming up with the devil. Nevertheless, this alignment was precisely what was required of the leadership, and with the worst enemies of the Arab nation, in order to liberate one part of the

Arab homeland from the forceful embrace of another. A verita-ble nightmare in every way!

At the crux, little split occurred in the Arab world. Normally, the Arabs would be divided along more or less natural and traditional lines of political interest and geography. Characteristically, for example, Iraq would be opposed by Syria, in light of the natural rivalry between the two countries, and also because of the tension between the two ruling Ba'th parties, which dominates the political life of these two regional powers. By contrast, Jordan would be on the side of the Iraqis for fear of the Syrians, and also in light of the traditional ties between the former and Iraq. And so on and so forth.

In the event, only Jordan broke the ranks of Arab unity in a substantial way. All the other Arab countries either joined in the effort against Iraq, or supported it, at least on the verbal level. Ultimately, as we know, the participation of Egyptian and Syrian forces in the fight against Iraq became an important fact of life for the international system, although it also constrained the abilities of the coalition. Evidentially, for instance, an invasion into Iraq itself which tried to change the regime there would be considered as a grave danger to other Arab regimes in the region, and, in light of this danger, among other considerations, an invasion with such a purpose would not be acceptable to the Arab countries. Thus, in practical terms, such an invasion would dissolve the entire Arab participation, hence putting in danger the international legitimacy of the officially sanctioned military effort. In short, the Arab participation was reversible. Thus Egypt and Syria joined in the limited effort to liberate Kuwait, and afterwards simply quit the coalition, the latter continuing to operate in constraining the sovereignty of Iraq, both on the ground and in the air.

For the Western powers in general and for the United States in particular, the political participation of key Arab powers in the coalition, and their fairly active role in sending military forces to the battlefield, were of critical importance, allowing the West to argue that the expedition was not one of the West against the Arabs, but rather one of liberating one of the Arab lands, with the consent and participation of the Arabs themselves. Once the war was conducted from the territory of Saudi Arabia, with the participation of Kuwaiti pilots, as well as Egyptian and Syrian troops, seemingly a true partnership existed between the Arabs and the West, something that had not been seen before in history. One might well wonder whether such an exceptional state of affairs will ever be encountered again in the foreseeable future.

The danger of this coalition falling apart appeared from two sources. One of these has already been referred to: the expansion of the war objectives beyond the expulsion of Iraq from Kuwait might have led to the shattering of the entire web of relations inside the fragile coalition. Here lies a partial answer to the question why the Americans did not drive on to Baghdad and try to get rid of Saddam and his entire regime. In addition, a second danger to the coalition was that of drawing Israel into the war. The political realities of the time did allow – but just – a coalition of Arabs with the West to fight the Iraqi conquest of Kuwait, but they would not have allowed a coalition which included Israel in the fight against Iraq, a key Arab country and one of the most vocal and active supporters of Arab causes in general, and radical Arab causes in particular. The consequences should Israel participate were understood by all, Arabs and non-Arabs alike. Thus, the Iraqis made every effort to draw or provoke Israel into the war. So they fired their surface-to-surface missiles into Israel, not because they hoped for any real damage, but because they hoped for a forceful Israeli retaliation, whose response in turn would have allowed them to define the war as one of the Arabs against Israel. In such a case, the Egyptians and the Syrians, and of course also the Saudis, would have faced an almost impossible situation. But fortunately for them, the damage caused in Israel by the Iraqi missiles was not severe enough to draw Israel into the war, although a significant segment of the leadership in Israel was sorely tempted to do exactly that: on a number of occasions, the Israeli forces were reportedly on the brink of initiating a military action which might have changed the patterns and the course of the war.

As these two dangers were avoided, the Arab countries could join the coalition and stay within it, at least until the original purpose of driving the Iraqis out of Kuwait was accomplished. If initially the Americans had seriously contemplated expanding the mission to get rid of the regime of Saddam, the Arab members of the coalition would have brought the coalition down. They would have had little choice, because the rulers of countries like Syria, and even Egypt, would not have been able to participate in an act that might have reflected on the legitimacy of their own regimes, and might also have called their survival into question.

For after all, the regime in power in Syria at the time was not so very different from the one in Iraq. And therefore, no reason existed for the then ruler of Damascus to help bring down the ruler of Baghdad in the name of ideologies that were promoted by the sword of foreigners. So that was one major reason for the coalition terminating the war when it did, at a time when many observers in Israel and the West expected, and hoped for, the continuation of the operation until Baghdad was taken and the regime of Saddam terminated.

Thus, one major consequence of the limited war has been that Saddam has survived, albeit with great difficulty. True, he was defeated on the battlefield. True, his country has since been punished by the international community's imposition of a devastating embargo, by having to put up with international arms inspection on its territory (at least until 1998), by relinquishing control to a large extent of significant chunks of its own territory, so that an internationally protected Kurdish zone now exists in the north and the no-fly zone to some extent protects the Shi'ites in the south.

Still, the regime remains intact, and its ruler still presides in person. This survival enables Saddam to argue, with some effect, that he did not lose the war. For him, the war continues, while his enemies are gone: Bush, Thatcher, others in the West. Asad of Syria is dead. The countries in the Gulf are not much better protected now than they were at the time, and they still depend on outside patrons. Iraq remains the dominant power in the region, along, of course, with neighbouring Iran.

To repeat, crucially Saddam has been able to remain effectively in power, although many of us have difficulties understanding why. Here are some apparent reasons: the man is most adroit and shrewd when it comes to political manipulations; he is most careful, cautious and methodical when it comes to his personal safety; his security apparatus has been very devoted and effective; his opposition has been disunited, disorganized and lacks central leadership; outside forces have been half-hearted about removing Saddam, fearing that the country might degenerate into chaos, fall apart and in general threaten the stability of the other countries in the Middle East. The central meaning of Saddam's survival is clear. The rules of the inter-Arab game judge the results of operations in light of one major criterion, which is simply the survival of the regime. And on that score, Saddam has been winning, and seems to be winning still.

On a more theoretical level of generalization about the inter-Arab system, what are the lessons of the conduct and of the consequences of the Gulf War? First, this system still has only limited uses. For there are major problems it cannot handle because of the lack of proper institutions, because it cannot make decisions that are not unanimous and because of a lack of consensus on the basic values of the system.

In this situation, where it is not possible to handle problems of military intervention on the basis of collective decision-making, two possibilities remain. A country with some strong allies might act on its own, as the Egyptians did in Yemen, or else it must appeal for help from forces outside the Arab world. The Gulf case is absolutely unique in that the latter case prevailed openly, in a major and visible way. However, to mix the exception with the rule would be a mistake. The rule is for the Arab nations to try to find solutions within the Arab family, and, when there are no solutions, it is better to live with no solutions than with one that reflects so badly on the entire Arab world. The fact is that neither before nor since the invasion of Kuwait and its aftermath has there been a single case remotely approximating this situation. And it is not easy to imagine similar situations in the future.

On the contrary, the countries contemplating aggression in the future will presumably operate in ways that will avoid the blatant mistakes of Saddam. At present, too, Middle Eastern countries seem to follow this guideline: the Syrians in Lebanon, for example, are most careful, as they have always been, to follow procedures that seem to give them a modicum of international legitimacy, on both the regional and global levels, so that their actions will not be equated with the adventures of Saddam Hussein.

The agenda of the inter-Arab system has not changed all that much, after all. The desperate attempts of Saddam to involve Israel in the conflict made eminent sense. For to repeat, in all probability it would not have been possible for the Arabs to fight Iraq had that country been engaged in active war with Israel.

The agenda of the inter-Arab system still revolves around some clear and well-established axes: unity, leadership, ideological differences, territorial issues between given countries, conflict with Israel, relationships with outside powers.

Certain trade-offs take place between these sets of issues, for it is possible to pursue aggressively one and to give in on another. When regime survival is at stake, for example, one can compromise on almost everything else other than the verbal commitments to the accepted slogans of the Arab world. But in the particular case of Iraq and the Gulf War, the Iraqis themselves made a huge mistake by blatantly attacking the principles of the system, while at the same time also attacking the concrete and vital interests of other countries inside and outside the Arab world. They thus could be punished because of the limited goals of the military operations aimed at Iraq. However, had these operations violated more of the established principles of the system, such as the overthrow of Saddam, the coalition would have fallen apart as far as the Arabs were concerned. And so the Iraqis tried to facilitate this dissolution by involving Israel in the conflict. Had that attempt succeeded, the Arab countries only with great difficulty could have continued to operate within the coalition, which probably would have just dissolved.

We need to have a sense of perspective. Just as it makes no sense to attribute to the inter-Arab system magic qualities that make it terribly important and dominant in the region, so also it makes little sense to underestimate its existence and potential importance. True, the practical abilities of the Arab states to cooperate in complex operations on a regional level are still quite limited, and are likely to remain so in the foreseeable future, for basic reasons that have to do with the very structure of the Arab states. But these limitations do not mean that the inter-Arab system is dead. For the idea of Arabism, with everything that it entails, is still attractive to a generation of younger radicals and intellectuals in the Arab world at large. And alternative ideologies (socialism, for example) are either dead, or strongly tied to the very idea of Arab nationalism, as in the case of radical Islam or the remnants of various leftist systems of thought in the region. Furthermore, were there to be a strong outside stimulus (as in the case of a possible massive confrontation with Israel), the inter-Arab system might come alive with greater force than at present as an alternative to each regime having to cope individually with the pressures of its public and of the various interested political movements and forces inside the various countries. Thus, in the final analysis, while the case of the Gulf War is extreme, and is not likely to be repeated, its very extremeness shows in sharp contours the nature and the limits of the inter-Arab system as a whole.

SELECTED BIBLIOGRAPHY

Bahgat, G., 'The Iraqi Crisis in the New Millennium: The Prospects', *Asian Affairs*, 87, 2 (June 2000), pp. 149–59.

Bassey, C.O., 'The Legitimation of Intervention Through Collective Security Regime: Some Policy Implications of the Gulf War', *African Journal of International Affairs and Development*, 5, 1 (June 2000), pp. 117–48.

Ben-Dor, G., 'Arab Rationality and Deterrence', in A. Klieman and A. Levite (eds), *Deterrence in the Middle East* (Tel Aviv: Jerusalem Post for the Jaffee Center for Strategic Studies, 1993).

Bush, G. and Scowcroft, B., *A World Transformed* (New York: Alfred A. Knopf, 1998).

Cordesman, A.H., *Kuwait: Recovery and Security after the Gulf War* (Boulder, CO: Westview Press, 1997).

Feldman, S., 'Israeli Deterrence and the Gulf War', in Efraim Inbar, *Strategic Consequences of the Gulf War for Israel*, Mideast Security and Policy Studies, 12 (Ramat-Gan: The BESA Center for Strategic Studies, Bar-Ilan University, 1993).

Lake, D.A., 'Ulysses' Triumph: American Power and the New World Order', *Security Studies*, 8, 4 (Summer 1999), pp. 44–78.

Levran, A., *Israeli Strategy after Desert Storm: Lessons of the Second Gulf War* (London and Portland, OR: Frank Cass, 1997).

Sadri, H.A., 'An Islamic Perspective on Non-Alignment: Iranian Foreign Policy in Theory and Practice', *Journal of Third World Studies*, 16, 2 (Fall 1999), pp. 29–46.

Part III:
Israel

4

Israel and the Gulf War

EFRAIM INBAR

INTRODUCTION

Iraq, under the leadership of Saddam Hussein, invaded Kuwait on 2 August 1990. It was a bold attempt on the part of Saddam Hussein to challenge the regional order and to assert his hegemony over the Middle East. Iraq's military power (whose army ranked at that time as the fifth largest in the world), in combination with the newly acquired riches of oil-producing Kuwait, could have catapulted Iraq to the leadership position in the Arab world. Moreover, the Iraqi control of its own oil reserves and Kuwait's, as well as its ability to threaten Saudi Arabian oil fields, could have granted Baghdad a major role in the world oil market (56 per cent of world proved reserves), enhancing further its regional aspirations and importance.[1]

Iraq's conquest of Kuwait, with the potential upgrading of its national might and of its regional status, also constituted a significant security challenge for Israel. Iraq has always been a bitter enemy of Israel and had even sent expeditionary forces to fight in all Arab wars against Israel (1948, 1967 and 1973). In contrast to Israel's immediate neighbors, it never signed any type of armistice agreement and continued to consider itself in a state of war with the 'Zionist State'. Iraq's leader was notorious for his vitriolic statements against Israel.[2] As recently as April 1990, Saddam Hussein had threatened 'to burn half of Israel' with chemical weapons.[3] His threats had a ring of credibility because prior to the August invasion he had deployed launchers of Scud-

C missiles to west Iraq, capable of carrying warheads to Israel. Moreover, Saddam was widely believed to be waiting for an appropriate opportunity to take revenge on Israel for its successful destruction of the Iraqi nuclear research reactor near Baghdad in June 1981, which was instrumental in delaying for a considerable time the fruition of the Iraqi nuclear program.

This chapter analyzes the Israeli responses to the new Iraqi challenge. The following pages review Israel's behavior during the crisis and analyze how Jerusalem coped with the dilemmas presented by the subsequent US-led Desert Storm Operation, which started on 17 January 1991. The final section deals with several strategic implications of the 1990–91 events for Israel.

THE PREWAR PERIOD

The invasion of Kuwait gave rise to grave concern in Jerusalem, as it could constitute a substantial change in Israel's geostrategic envelope and as it confirmed the Israeli prognosis of the harsh Middle Eastern realities, which are not easily conducive to peaceful coexistence. It definitely reinforced the high threat perceptions of the Yitzhak Shamir-led right-wing government, the most hawkish in Israel's political history (installed in June 1990).

The Initial Reaction

Initially, the occupation of Kuwait was seen as a *fait accompli*, which the international community would hardly be prepared to challenge. Skepticism about the power of the economic sanctions to move Saddam into surrendering Kuwait was widespread. Israelis perceived the deployment of American troops to Saudi Arabia primarily as a defensive move intended to deter Iraq from invading Saudi Arabia and its oil fields in the northeast. At the end of August, Shamir was pessimistic about the outcome of the efforts to resolve the Gulf crisis by diplomatic means.[4] The initially strong American stand against Saddam's aggression was somewhat of a pleasant surprise for the Israeli government. Yet, the American commitment to use force to liberate Kuwait was questioned throughout the crisis. In the last days of 1990, Israeli Defense Minister Moshe Arens still believed that even the slightest gesture on the part of Saddam towards a partial withdrawal would cause President George Bush to delay any military action.[5]

Within a short time of the Iraqi invasion, Israelis realized that their country might also become a target in the framework of the ambitious Iraqi hegemonic quest, or in response to an American attack on Iraqi targets. Iraqi aggression against Israel became more likely as the crisis evolved. President Bush was successful in creating international consensus against Iraqi occupation of Kuwait during the autumn of 1990; he imposed economic sanctions on Iraq and mustered legitimacy for an increased American military presence in the Gulf and for the possible use of military force to evict the Iraqi troops from Kuwait.

Initially, the diversion of attention from the intractable Israeli–Palestinian conflict was a relief for Israel. However, it was short-lived. While the USA assembled an international coalition, Iraq attempted to weaken it, by linking the solution to the occupation of Kuwait to a resolution of the disputed territories in the Israeli–Syrian and Israeli–Palestinian conflicts. Championing the Palestinian cause gained support in the streets of the Arab world, as did additional Iraqi threats against Israel. The Iraqi threats gradually became more strident and were accompanied by missile tests, which were supposed to demonstrate not only intentions to harm Israel, but also capabilities.

The great popularity of Saddam in the streets of Arab cities all over the Arab world further heightened Israeli threat perception. The general acclaim to Saddam's anti-Israeli rhetoric, in contrast to his brutal dictatorship and poor governance record, triggered among Israelis the 'evoked set' concept that the Arabs are basically intent on destroying the Jewish state.[6] Yet, the Israeli perceptions of grave danger as a result of the emergence of a mighty Iraq capable of manipulating Gulf oil and petrodollars for imperial schemes were shared by its Arab neighbors. The fears that the Iraqi army might march into Saudi Arabia existed also in Washington.[7] Israel hoped that the convergence of many national interests inside and outside the Arab world would prevent Iraqi hegemony in the Gulf region, which had

wider implications for future Middle East politics and align-
ments.[8] Yet, the determination of the USA to check Iraqi revi-
sionism, which is now a known fact, was then often doubted
until the war broke out on 17 January 1991.

Israel also harbored suspicions that it would have to foot the
bill for the building and maintaining of the coalition, by being
pressured by the USA to make concessions to the Arabs after
the crisis ended. In addition, it feared that the American arms
sales to Arab states would erode the balance of power. When the
USA announced its intention to sell advanced weapons to Saudi
Arabia, a country not at peace with Israel, the Israeli government faced the dilemma of opposing Washington on the US
arms deals or accepting them and settling for a compensation,
thereby minimizing tensions with the Bush administration.

Israeli Policies

The day after the conquest of Kuwait, Prime Minister Yitzhak
Shamir convened a small informal group for consultations
(including Arens, the IDF Chief of Staff, Lieutenant-General
Dan Shomron, and a few ministers close to the Prime Minister),
which revolved around the question of the inevitability of an
Iraqi–Israeli clash. Shamir believed that Saddam sought to
engage Israel in hostilities in order to break out of his isolation
and score points in the inter-Arab competition for a leadership
role. Therefore, Shamir preferred a low-profile policy in order
not to provide an easy pretext for Iraqi aggression and not to
complicate the American efforts to defend Saudi Arabia. This
preference became the dominant feature of the Israeli policy
until after the end of the Gulf War.[9]

Israel favored a wide American military attack to devastate
Iraqi conventional might, as well as its chemical capabilities and
nuclear program, believed at the time to be anywhere between
two and five years from completion. Therefore, Jerusalem went
along with the American preferences for keeping Israel unin-
volved and promised Washington not to use the crisis for pre-
emptive measures against Iraqi facilities. Shamir reiterated his
complete endorsement of US policy on the Gulf crisis and

expressed readiness to help militarily, if necessary, although he was content to maintain the low-profile policy.[10]

From mid-August, the Israeli Air Force (IAF) and its air defense system were put on increasing levels of alert to intercept Iraqi planes as the war became nearer.[11] Throughout the crisis, the IDF started planning and training for complicated missions to deal with Iraqi missile launchers. However, it became very clear that carrying out such missions required coordination with the American air force, needed because Israel preferred not to cross Jordanian airspace and fight the Jordanians in order to attain air superiority, which would jeopardize the coalition's cohesion and the stability of the Hashemite regime.[12] Instead, Israel wanted to fly through Saudi airspace, whose tacit permission for transit could be secured only through Washington.

The Israeli military intelligence also set up a special group of psychologists to prepare a psychological profile of Saddam in order to predict whether he would attack Israel. The classified report, which came to the conclusion that Saddam was just waiting for a pretext to attack Israel and that he had no restraints whatsoever, except considerations relating to his own survival, was challenged within the intelligence community and also by the CIA, and was, therefore, not accepted as a working assumption.[13]

Parallel to the preparations for retaliation, Israel deliberately attempted to enhance its deterrence by issuing several public warnings by senior ministers.[14] In August, Yitzhak Shamir warned, 'Anybody that will attempt to attack Israel will bring upon himself a terrible catastrophe.'[15] A month later, he said that Israel took Iraq's threats seriously, and warned that it would strike back.[16] Similarly, Arens declared in November that Israel's reaction to an Iraqi attack would not be 'low profile'.[17] In December, Foreign Minister David Levy warned Iraq that, in case of aggression against Israel, the response would be very determined,[18] while Arens stated in January 1991 that, if attacked, 'Israel will not hesitate to respond.'[19]

The Iraqi chemical weapons' potential was of particular concern to Israel, although it had no conclusive evidence that Iraq had chemical warheads' for its missiles. Despite the realization that Saddam had used chemical weapons against adversaries during the Iran–Iraq War (1980–88), Arens offered on several occasions evaluations stating that Iraq did not have the chemical warheads for missiles; that its ability to cause great damage to Israel was limited; and that there was only a small likelihood of an Iraqi chemical attack on Israel. Arens decided initially against giving out gas masks to the civilian population in order to prevent the creation of panic and not to signal to Saddam that Israel took chemical attacks into consideration. Yet, on 19 August, David Levy demanded that the Ministry of Defense hand out gas masks, a task which was complicated by the inadequate availability of gas masks, particularly for children. Israel hurriedly purchased such items in Europe. The government gave in to popular pressure and, on 7 October, started providing masks to citizens living in the urban centers. Later on, the Ministry of Defense responded to public demands and distributed masks also to the rural areas.[20] In general, by the end of the five months' interval until the war broke out the civil population was better prepared for chemical warfare.[21] Following the failure of the meeting between US Secretary of State James Baker and Iraqi Foreign Minister Tariq Aziz, on 9 January 1991, Israel upgraded its preparations for chemical warfare. It mobilized reserve civil defense units and launched a multi-language public educational campaign (in Hebrew, Arabic, Russian and Amharic). The government instructed the citizens to carry their gas masks at all times and to prepare a sealed room in their homes in case of a chemical attack.

As the 15 January deadline approached and war became increasing likely, Israeli concerns about Iraqi aggression increased correspondingly. The premise of Arens was that the prospects for missile attacks on Israel would grow following an American attack on Iraq.[22] Indeed, when the Iraqi Foreign Minister was asked whether US military action against his country would lead to an attack on Israel, he replied, 'Yes. Absolutely yes.'[23] On 15 January, the government decided to close the schools from the next day onwards as a precautionary move.

72

The Jordanian Angle

Jordan's relations with Israel were more often than not characterized by tacit strategic cooperation against Palestinian nationalism and the hegemonic impulses emanating from Cairo,
Damascus or Baghdad. Yet, weak Jordan had to play a fine-tuned
balancing act in the intra-Arab arena.[24] From the outset of the
1990 crisis, Israel feared that Iraqi–Jordanian military cooperation would expand and Jordan would not be able to resist the
pressure to become the staging area for a land and/or artillery
attack on Israel. Jordan allowed Iraqi warplanes, painted with
Jordanian colors, to conduct reconnaissance and photographing
missions along the Israeli border. Iraqi planes took pictures of the
Israeli nuclear reactor at Dimona. Moreover, high-level Iraqi
field officers toured the border and the possible invasion routes
into Israel. Jordan's proximity to Israel's population centers
turned the Hashemite Kingdom into a key component of a puta-
tive eastern front. The possibility of deployment of Iraqi forces
along the Jordan River became a serious Israeli concern after the
Iraqi invasion of Kuwait.

Arens had already conveyed such apprehensions to the USA
in July 1990. Arens and others within the Israeli security establishment also feared that King Hussein would not be able to
withstand popular pressures, as had happened prior to the June
1967 war, and would actively side with Saddam Hussein in operations against Israel.[25] Moreover, Shamir believed that the
Jordanian involvement in a war on Iraq's side would put an end
to the Hashemite Kingdom.[26] Therefore, Shamir instructed
Arens to state that the entrance of Iraqi troops into Jordan
would constitute a 'red line', which in Israeli strategic parlance
meant a *casus belli*. From the Knesset podium on 6 August,
Arens unequivocally warned against Iraqi military presence in
Jordan. Moreover, the Israeli Prime Minister conveyed the same
message to President Bush and to the Jordanians.[27] As Jordan's
alignment with Iraq became clearer during the first months after
the invasion and as it helped Iraq overcome the American-led
economic boycott, Israel's concerns grew. Indeed, in December
1990, David Levy warned Jordan once more against allowing its

territory or airspace to be used for launching an Iraqi assault on Israel.[28] In response to the Israeli concerns and because of fears of an Israeli attempt to destabilize his kingdom, King Hussein called for a secret meeting with Shamir in London, on 5 January 1991.[29] He wanted an Israeli promise to refrain from using Jordanian territory and airspace in its struggle against Iraq. Shamir agreed, on condition that the Jordanian army would prevent Iraqi flights in its airspace and that all military cooperation between Amman and Baghdad would end. Shamir's only caveat to Hussein was that Israel would not be bound by their agreement in case of an Iraqi invasion of Jordan.[30]

US–Israeli Relations

Prior to the Kuwait invasion, relations between Jerusalem and Washington were marred by the reluctance of Israel's government to go along with the American suggestions for negotiating an agreement with the Palestinians, which would bring an end to the Palestinian uprising (intifada). The Bush administration attempted to pressure Israel to change its settlement policy in Judea and Samaria by withholding the grant of US-guaranteed loans for the absorption of the Soviet immigrants, who were arriving by the hundreds of thousands, mostly practically destitute. In July, it also delayed talks on strategic cooperation between the two countries.[31]

The crisis, however, brought about an amelioration in US–Israeli relations, as the issues of dispute became secondary. Moreover, the USA wanted Israel to stay out of the crisis so as not to disrupt its fragile multi-national diplomatic and military effort with other Arab states in confronting Saddam. From the beginning of the crisis the USA urged Israel to refrain from action, which could complicate the US attempts to build a large coalition to back its diplomatic and, if necessary, military efforts, to restore the status quo ante in Kuwait. Washington wanted to decouple the Gulf crisis from the Arab–Israeli nexus, which suited Israeli interests. This American preference assumed that Israeli involvement in the conflict might increase Arab support for Iraq and even lead to desertion of the US-led coalition by several Arab states (Syria most likely). Baker wrote, 'Throughout the prewar period, keeping Israel out of the conflict had been a central strategic concern of our diplomacy.'[32] The USA was afraid that an Iraqi attack on Israel would weaken the Arabs' willingness to ally themselves with the USA, despite their interest in seeing Iraq crushed.

The USA continuously demanded reassurances from the Israeli leadership that it would not pre-empt. Shamir, during his December visit to Washington, repeated personally Israel's pledge to Bush, not to make pre-emptive moves. When asked of the Israeli response to an attack, Shamir responded that Israel would defend itself and would consult with the USA, but was careful not to promise that he would seek permission to use force.[33]

Israel, which had marketed itself as a strategic asset, found itself outside the military contingency plans of the USA. Bush and Baker visited the Middle East and met Arab leaders, but omitted Israel from their itinerary. Israel felt it was not treated like an ally.[34] Israel wanted access to American intelligence on Iraq and operational coordination between the US military and the IDF to deal effectively with various contingencies.[35] Coordination with the American air force was sought in particular, because Israel feared that before the coalition acted Saddam would hit Israel, or the coalition would fail in eliminating the Scud missiles' threat. It believed that it could do a good job fighting the missiles with the Americans or alone. Moreover, Israel wanted to prove its value as an ally. The USA continuously reassured Israel that the coalition would deal effectively with the targets in west Iraq that threatened Israel and refused to establish a coordination mechanism.[36]

Israel made several requests for access to real-time intelligence from US satellites, but was turned down.[37] Israel was also originally left out of the Operation Desert Storm supplemental foreign aid package. It was disappointed also because it was not included among the 'front line' states, which became eligible for compensation by the Gulf Crisis Financial Coordination Group (chaired by the USA). In September, Arens requested money and weapons from a reluctant administration that agreed to offer two batteries of Patriot surface-to-air missiles (SAMs), 12 to 15 surplus F-15s and ammunition for artillery and tanks in order to secure Israeli cooperation.[38] In December, Shamir requested mechanisms for better communication and only in January was a special secure telephone line, code-named 'Hammer Rick', established between Secretary of Defense Richard Cheney and Arens to allow better warning of incoming missiles. In January, the USA also offered to deploy in Israel US-manned Patriots, but Arens refused because he did not want a precedent of foreign forces participating in the defense of Israel, although this is ultimately what happened.[39]

Public warnings by David Levy in early January that an Iraqi attack would be considered an act of war and would prompt terrible retribution elicited concerns in Washington, and the President sent to Israel two top officials, who were particularly trusted by the Israelis, Deputy Secretary of State Lawrence Eagleburger and Under-Secretary of Defense for Policy Paul Wolfowitz, to urge restraint.[40] As Shamir was not ready to commit himself to refrain from reaction to Iraqi aggression and continued to demand coordination with the USA, Eagleburger suggested that in case Israel was determined to proceed with an attack it would consult with the USA so that a certain area in Iraq would be cleared of US military presence ('deconflicting'), to prevent any collision of forces, an idea to which Shamir agreed. Eagleburger clarified that the USA was not ready to cooperate militarily with Israel and would not transfer information on targets, or secure flight rights over Arab countries, but was ready to vacate an agreed area in accordance with Israel.[41] This understanding would have allowed the USA additional time to exert influence on Israel to refrain in case it decided to act unilaterally.

ISRAEL'S BEHAVIOR DURING THE GULF WAR

On 18 January, at 2 a.m., sirens woke Israel's citizens following an Iraqi missile attack. Throughout the war, Israel was subjected to 39 missiles causing directly only two fatalities, plus a few hundred wounded. Most damage was done to property, with thousands of buildings damaged. The economy was paralyzed for the duration of the war. Israel, for the first time, was at war only with a faraway country, with which it did not share a border. It was also the first time that its population centers were the main target of the enemy. Another first was Israel's decision to refrain from reacting to attacks on its soil and citizens.

Maintaining the Military Option

The day after the first missiles hit Israel, Prime Minister Shamir called for a cabinet meeting, at which the IDF presented several options for military reaction. During the discussion, Arens pointed out two main constraints on any Israeli military initiative: the great distance to the chosen targets and the lack of adequate intelligence. Arens also feared that an Israeli raid without American coordination would be risky and would increase casualties.[42] As noted, no photographs were supplied by the USA and the IAF did not carry out any aerial reconnaissance flight over west Iraq. Ariel Sharon suggested sending planes to take pictures and informing the USA of the mission. Shamir obtained the approval of the cabinet for the plans to attack targets in west Iraq and to get more intelligence, contingent upon coordination with Washington.[43] As more Scuds fell on Israel, the pressure from the senior military echelons, particularly the air force, on the political level to approve action in west Iraq increased.[44] Dan Shomron advocated restraint, however.[45] Shamir used Shomron's advocacy to balance the more hawkish elements in his coalition government. However, the main factor in deciding between Israeli action and restraint was probably the American diplomacy.[46]

Looking back at the crisis, Shamir admitted in his memoirs that the decision to refrain from action in response to Iraq's missile attacks was the most difficult in his life and the one most opposed to his principles and ideology.[47] According to Shamir's analysis, Israel had three options: unilateral use of the IAF to search for missiles and to destroy them; reliance on the USA to do the job; and the preferred one of a military reaction in cooperation with the USA. The USA conveyed its opposition to the first and last options. Unilateral action would have involved the violation of Jordanian airspace. The likely Jordanian opposition could have been easily overcome militarily, but the diplomatic significance of Israeli–Jordanian exchanges could have brought about a break-up of the coalition. Shamir did not want to be blamed for that and for missing an opportunity to put an end to Saddam's regime. Moreover, Shamir's promise to King Hussein in January 1991 was an additional constraint on Israel's desire for action during the Gulf War. Finally, Shamir's personality, which seemed averse to making bold decisions, blended well with the policy of restraint.

The Israeli calculus of the use of force during the crisis was influenced primarily by two main factors: the way the Americans dealt with the Iraqi threat and the extent of the threat for Israel.[48] Although there was dissatisfaction with the way in which the coalition dealt with the missile threat, the Israelis were pleased to see the Iraqi army quashed. Moreover, despite the political and strategic inconvenience of not reacting to missile attacks, the limited number of casualties did not constitute enough of an incentive to order a high-risk punitive mission to Iraq. Shamir did not see even the possibility of attacks with chemical warheads as an existential threat, although, as was conveyed to the Americans, it would have triggered an Israeli military response.[49] The military risks also dissuaded the Israelis from retaliation.

Nevertheless, Israel was very close to retaliation. Arens approached Washington for satellite pictures of west Iraq, as well as to arrange an air corridor above Saudi Arabia. While his wishes were not granted, by 1 February, the IDF readied a plan for an air and commando raid in west Iraq, commencing the training of several units for this particular mission. On several occasions, Israeli pilots sat in their cockpits on the runways waiting for a 'green light' from the political level, which failed to come.

Technical problems also delayed the decision to act. For example, at one cabinet meeting Major-General Avihu Bin-Nun, Chief of the IAF, reported that weather conditions in west Iraq did not permit the use of the IAF for at least two to three days.[50] By mid-February, Arens made further inquiries with the intelligence as to the likely Jordanian response to the use of its airspace by Israeli jetfighters and was told that the Jordanians would definitely try to intercept them. The IDF intelligence officers also discouraged Arens from the idea of testing the Jordanians by sending an airplane or a helicopter. However, Arens believed that, at that stage in the war, King Hussein had become more reluctant to identify Jordan as an Iraqi ally and would tolerate Israeli activity in its skies.[51] The IAF submitted to Arens on 26 February an acceptable profile of a test flight over Jordanian airspace, but Shamir refused to approve it because he thought the war would be soon over and such a flight would only create unnecessary risks. Arens tried again the next day with Shamir, this time successfully. He also contacted Cheney to secure US approval for a larger raid, but was told that such a matter had to be discussed at the highest level, between the President and the Prime Minister. The planned flight was delayed by weather conditions and on 28 February the war ended, without any action, which struck Arens as a terrible blow for Israel's deterrence.[52] It is quite possible that, had the war continued a few days longer, resulting in a higher casualty count of Israelis, we might have seen Israeli soldiers hunting missile launchers in Iraq. Actually, on counterfactual inquiry, had events developed slightly differently, Israeli lack of retaliation strikes was still not a foregone conclusion.[53] In other words, pure luck played an important role in Israeli restraint.[54]

The USA and Israel

Throughout the war, the USA used the 'secure line' to provide Israel with information about incoming missiles, as its satellite picked up the Iraqi launches. This allowed Israel to activate its civil warning system, which allowed Israel's citizens a few minutes to prepare for the worst. Immediately after the first missile attack, Arens conveyed to Baker, as well as to Cheney, Israel's desire to react militarily. In his autobiography, Arens quotes his words to Baker: 'We don't have a choice … they have hit us. We have to hit them back. Israel can't sit here and be hit with missiles and do nothing.'[55] On the same day, Shamir cautioned Baker in a similar vein: 'This is a terrible problem for us, which we have to face up to … Israel has never failed to respond.'[56]

After the war started, the US decision-making process oper-
ated under the assumption that Israeli restraint was reversible.
Indeed, 'there were few things the President and his top aides
worried about more' than the problem of keeping Israel out of
the war.[57] Chairman of the Joint Chiefs of Staff General Colin
Powell referred to the issue as 'the supersensitive need to keep
Israel out of the fight'.[58] Yet, the USA had reason to believe that
Israel would hesitate to retaliate. According to Baker's memoirs,
he evaluated that Israel would have insurmountable difficulties
in acting without the coalition forces 'deconflicting', i.e. halting
flying missions in a certain area, thus allowing Israel a corridor
for its airplanes. Alternatively, Israel could act if it acquired from
the USA the electronic identification codes of the coalition
warplanes, to prevent inadvertent clashes between Israeli and
coalition pilots. The USA had no intention of doing either.[59] The
USA refused also to comply with Israel's demands for an electronic downlink to US intelligence satellites (to have real-time
information on Iraqi deployments), a direct communications
channel to General Norman Schwartzkopf's headquarters or a
liaison officer dispatched to the Central Command staff.

The general feeling that Israel was not treated as an ally and
that the USA was not sensitive enough to its security needs was
reinforced during the war.[60] Arens, when briefed by the USA at
the beginning of the war, was not convinced of the seriousness of
the American efforts in dealing with the Scud missiles. He came
to the conclusion that the USA would definitely fail to meet the
challenge in 24 hours as promised. Senior IDF officers com-
plained that the USA gave only sketchy information about its
anti-Scud activities in west Iraq and refused to detail the ways of
its operational aspects.[61] During the war, Lieutenant-General
Shomron expressed disappointment at the American achievements in this area.[62] Major-General Bin-Nun was less diplomatic when he said that the USA did not even try to stop the
launching of Scuds toward Israel and claimed that his forces
could have done a much better job of disabling the Scuds.[63]

After being attacked by missiles armed with conventional
warheads there was growing concern in Jerusalem that Iraq
might use chemical warheads as well. The Iraqi threat to use 'as

yet unused weapons' increased the Israeli threat perception. The remark made by John Sununu, Chief of Staff at the White House, that such a contingency would not necessarily lead to nuclear retaliation was not well received in Jerusalem. Arens called Cheney and lodged a complaint.[64]

Moreover, the USA rejected the initial Israeli plea for emergency assistance in loans and grants presented by Arens to Baker in the course of their 11 February meeting. Washington believed that it was doing Israel a favor by destroying the Iraqi army and that Israel should therefore not be compensated for its restraint. Nevertheless, Washington tried to impress Israel with its awareness of its dilemma and communicated much sympathy and appreciation for the Israeli stand. US-manned batteries of Patriot surface-to-air missiles were deployed in Israel, following Arens' request, in the false belief of the Americans and the Israelis that the Patriot missiles had a limited capability to intercept missiles (they failed to intercept even one Scud missile). The USA also decided to send Eagleburger once again to calm the Israelis; to convey agreement to increase the combat sorties to west Iraq against the Scuds; to approve limited operations by its special forces; to supply Israel with more intelligence information; and to allow Israeli intelligence officers to assist American officers with target identification.[65] The administration upgraded the intelligence sharing and was willing to incorporate Israeli suggestions for targeting. The quiet cooperation in the area of intelligence also allowed Israel to feel it made a contribution to the war effort.[66] Dick Cheney even tried to bolster the Israeli faltering deterrence. On 2 February, in response to a planted question at a press conference about Israeli possible response to Iraqi chemical attacks, he did not rule out an Israeli nuclear response, hoping such a statement would enhance Israeli deterrence.

The attempt to make American measures conditional on Jerusalem's restraint met with Israeli resistance and eventually the USA understood that American unconditional support measures helped Shamir resist his hawkish colleagues' pressure to retaliate.[67] Indeed, cabinet members such as Ariel Sharon, Yitzhak Modai and Rafael Eitan believed that Israel needed no coordination with the USA. Announcing Israel's resolution to act would force the USA *de facto* to create deconflicting. Arens was also surprised at Shamir's great reluctance to order an attack and to risk a confrontation with the Americans.[68] Yet, even Shamir's patience ended eventually and only a call from the President brought about the order to delay attack. Indeed, the constant American diplomatic contacts and pressure were effective.

Shamir was able to give in to American pressure also because the Israelis generally supported the policy of restraint of their government. In fact, about 94 per cent of the public felt that the government was handling the security situation either 'well' or 'very well'.[69] Even groups like 'Peace Now', as well as leftist intellectuals, who were usually critical of the government policies, issued calls to peace movements throughout the world to support Israel during the crisis.[70] This occurrence is in accordance with the findings of sociologists of war, such as George Simmel, who claim that external threat produces consensus.[71]

Another reason for Shamir's behavior was the international sympathy poured on Israel and its government. There were even examples of substantive benefits for Israel. Germany decided to give Israel large-scale aid, including the building of two submarines, whose procurement had been previously canceled for lack of funds. Germany also paid for one Patriot battery. Economic sanctions imposed by the European Union (EU) were also removed. Because he was seen as intransigent on the peace process, Shamir wished to improve Israel's image abroad and improve relations particularly with the American administration, hoping that Israel would be owed something for its forbearance. Basically, the Israeli government tried to make the best of a very awkward situation.

STRATEGIC IMPLICATIONS FOR ISRAEL

While the strategic significance of the 1991 Gulf War for Israel was greatly exaggerated,[72] it highlighted several components in Israel's strategic environment of the 1990s.[73]

The 1990–91 crisis demonstrated once more the importance

of systemic factors for the regional balance of power. The loosening of bipolarity in the international system, which was heralded in many quarters as the beginning of a new, more peaceful world order, had mixed effects on the Middle East. Unlike the European sub-system, this region had never been under rigid bipolar control by the two superpowers. The Soviet decline by 1990 further decreased Moscow's ability to constrain its Arab allies, thereby allowing countries like Syria and Iraq greater freedom of action. One factor accounting for the timing of the Iraqi military action in Kuwait was Gorbachev's reluctance to be drawn into Middle Eastern affairs.[74] Another systemic factor explaining the Iraqi move was the deterioration in the local balance of power in the Gulf. In the aftermath of the long Iran–Iraq War (1980–88), a weakened Iran was no longer capable of deterring an Iraqi conquest of Kuwait.

The Gulf War was an additional reminder to Arab elites that Israel was not necessarily the most dangerous enemy in the region. Moreover, it was a vivid example for a situation in which several Arab countries were de facto allied with Israel, this time against the hegemonic aspirations from Baghdad. Earlier, in the 1980s, the radical Islamic fervor from Tehran was seen in most Arab capitals as a dangerous development of greater security risk than the existence of Israel. Jerusalem shared the threat perception of the secular Arab elites. This perception of occasionally being in the same strategic boat is one component in the gradual acceptance of Israel as a fait accompli in the region.[75] This is one of the factors that facilitated the convening of the October 1991 Madrid Peace Conference. At this conference, for the first time, the majority of the Arab states, including Saudi Arabia and the Gulf sheikhdoms, were ready to participate in bilateral and/or multilateral dealings with Israel.

Indeed, the Gulf crisis showed once again that the Arab–Israeli conflict was just one among many in the conflict-ridden Middle East and that the Palestinian issue was not the most threatening to regional stability. Moreover, it indicated that the use of force was part and parcel of the Middle Eastern rules of the game. It also vividly demonstrated the dangers of the spread of weapons of mass destruction in the Middle East, which constituted for Israel an existential threat.

The seizure of Kuwait by Iraq and the subsequent events served as a test to US–Israeli relations. It showed the possible divergence of interests and questioned the assumption of Israel being a strategic asset in a changed international system. While the utility of allies in a unipolar world has declined somewhat, we know, in retrospect, that the bilateral relations remained very strong.

For Israel, the Gulf War constituted a painful reminder of the limitations to the freedom of action of small states in the international arena. Even if they have the capacity to act, as Israel did in the winter of 1991, quite often they have to take into consideration the wishes of great powers. This is particularly true in a situation where there is only one hegemonic power in the international system, which further curtails the freedom of action of small states.

The Gulf War was an additional reminder of the limitations of the Israeli intelligence apparatus and the possibility of a strategic surprise. Despite the fact that Israel's security establishment and its right-wing government had no illusions as to the aggressive nature of Saddam Hussein's regime, the move to take Kuwait surprised Jerusalem. The large investments in intelligence in place since the 1973 October War still did not prevent Israel being caught by surprise. US Secretary of State James Baker wrote in his memoirs that even the Israelis believed that Saddam's threats and military concentrations along the Kuwaiti border were designed only to secure economic concessions from the Kuwaitis.[76] Moreover, Israel was surprised that Saddam was serious about hitting Israeli targets. Israel's intelligence service, the Mossad, told US intelligence counterparts that Saddam's rhetoric was designed to deter an Israeli attack, not to threaten one of his own.[77] Likewise, the Iraqi nuclear progress was unforeseen in Jerusalem.[78]

The crisis in the Gulf was a sobering experience for the supporters of the idea that 'Jordan is Palestine', which was held by several people in key positions in Israel, including Ariel Sharon. According to this concept, Jordan, whose majority was of Palestinian origin, should be turned into a Palestinian state.

Enthroning Yasir Arafat, instead of Hashemite Hussein in Jordan, would in turn relieve much of the pressure from Israel to solve the Palestinian problem. The apprehension during the crisis about the weakness of the Hashemite regime taught the Israelis of the importance of having a friendly buffer state to the east. It was widely recognized that Jordan's territory became Israel's strategic depth.

The war renewed the Jordanian–Israeli understandings of mutual interest. Moreover, several months after the war ended Shamir made a point of impressing upon Baker the need for the generous support of the Hashemite Kingdom because of its importance for regional stability, despite King Hussein's alignment with Saddam during the war.[79] This eventually facilitated the signing of the October 1994 peace treaty between Jerusalem and Amman.

Many concluded that the Gulf War with its display of technological superiority was a good omen for Israel. They argued that Israel's highly advanced military force has a better chance to deter and/or overcome an Arab conventional onslaught. The so-called 'Revolution in Military Affairs' (RMA) was seen as assuring Israel's military superiority, justifying a lower Israeli threat perception. However, Israelis were usually more cautious in learning such a lesson. Their view of the RMA was more conservative. Israel has for years emphasized the importance of airpower and smart weapons and has developed an evolutionary approach to strategy and tactics. Moreover, Israel realized that its military arsenal was severely limited in size in comparison to the coalition's. Furthermore, Israel will probably not have at its disposal the time the allies had to operate freely in Iraq. Israeli strategists have been for years sensitized to the 'political clock' involved in military operation, which meant that their expectation was that there would be international pressure to stop their activities, particularly if they were on the winning side.

The Gulf War was a severe test to Israeli deterrence and it was only partially successful. While Israel seemed to deter an Iraqi missile attack armed with chemical weapons, it failed regarding conventional attacks on its population centers. Iraqi behavior demonstrated that, under certain – not necessarily unique – circumstances, Israeli threats might be ineffective.[80]

Surprisingly, the missile attacks are not universally accepted as a deterrence failure, although they were preceded by a series of explicit Israeli threats to retaliate against Iraq if the latter attacked Israel.[81] The deterrence failure was amplified by the Arab expectations that Israel would respond. According to General Schwartzkopf, King Fahd of Saudi Arabia in a conversation with Baker in November 1990 said 'he could not expect Israel to stand idly if attacked'.[82] Baker said in return: 'I had been able to secure agreements from all our Arab coalition partners that if Saddam attacked Israel first, and Israel struck back, they would remain firm.'[83] President Hosni Mubarak of Egypt and President Hafiz al-Asad of Syria made similar statements. Ex post facto, the Israeli decision to refrain from a military response received different interpretations in the Arab world. One major view was that Israel was weak militarily and/or its freedom of action was seriously hampered by American pressure.[84] Such a view could hardly reinforce Israeli deterrence.

The Iraqi missile attacks (with conventional warheads) resulted in only minimal casualties, but the economic damage was considerable as the country was paralyzed for several weeks. The Arabs observed that long-range surface-to-surface missiles (SSMs), such as the Scuds fired on Israel, were very useful politically and that their operation was not dependent upon having a modern military force. Even militarily strong countries such as Israel were vulnerable. Moreover, the allied air campaign to suppress Iraqi launches of Scud missiles against Israel, Saudi Arabia and other Persian Gulf nations during Desert Storm ran into many problems. While the launch rates generally declined over the course of the Gulf War, the intense efforts to find and destroy the missiles, particularly the mobile launchers, seem to have been unsuccessful, since they remained remarkably elusive and survivable.[85] The trend of acquiring SSMs by the Middle Eastern armies has indeed accelerated since the Gulf War.

The Israeli vulnerability was very obvious as thousands of Tel Aviv residents chose to move away to more peripheral areas of the country. The mayor of Tel Aviv at that time, Major-General (ret.) Shlomo Lahat, attacked them publicly and called them 'deserters'. This display of weakness led Israeli leaders, such as

Yitzhak Rabin, to believe that there was great urgency in reaching peace with Israel's neighbors even with greater concessions than had been planned.[86]

CONCLUSION

The 1991 Gulf War was a reminder of the vicissitudes of Middle Eastern politics, the vulnerability of Israel to missile attacks and the limits of Israeli military power and freedom of action. Israel's rational choice to act with much restraint during the war was mainly the product of auspicious coincidence and much luck. Following the war there were hopes, in Israel and elsewhere, for a new order in the Middle East, which, years later, we can testify as having remained unfulfilled. While the Gulf War was indeed an important event in international relations in the Middle East, the USA failed to impose a *Pax Americana* on the region for a variety of reasons, which are beyond the scope of this chapter. The Middle East remained a tough neighborhood.

NOTES

I thank Andrew Bacevich and Stuart Cohen for their useful comments on a previous draft.

1. Robert J. Lieber, 'Oil and Power After the Gulf War', *International Security*, 17, 1 (Summer 1992), pp. 160–2.
2. On his personality, see Efraim Karsh and Inari Rautsi, *Saddam Hussein: A Political Biography* (London: Brassey's, 1991).
3. FBIS Daily Report, Near East and South Asia, 3 April 1990, pp. 32–3.
4. *Jerusalem Post*, 27 August 1990, p. 1.
5. Moshe Arens, *Broken Covenant* (Hebrew; Tel Aviv: Yediot Aharonot, 1995), p. 163.
6. For the evoked set concept, see Robert Jervis, *Perception and Misperception in International Politics* (Princeton, NJ: Princeton University Press, 1976), pp. 213–16.
7. Arens, *Broken Covenant*, p. 163. For US apprehensions, see James A. Baker, III with Thomas M. DeFrank, *The Politics of Diplomacy: Revolution, War and Peace, 1989–1992* (New York: G.P. Putnam's Sons, 1995), pp. 277, 300.
8. For an analysis of the behavior of the Arab states during the crisis, see Bruce Maddy-Weitzman, 'Continuity and Change in the inter-Arab System', in Gad Barzilai, Aharon Klieman and Gil Shidlo (eds), *The Gulf Crisis and Its Global Aftermath* (London: Routledge, 1993), pp. 33–50.
9. Yitzhak Shamir, *Summing-Up* (Hebrew; Tel Aviv: Edanim, 1994), pp. 264–5, see also his interview to the *Jerusalem Post*, 23 August 1990, p. 1.
10. *Jerusalem Post*, 30 November 1990, p. 1. See also Arens, *Broken Covenant*, p. 162.
11. Arens, *Broken Covenant*, p. 163. See also Laura Zittrain Eisenberg, 'Passive

Belligerency: Israel and the 1991 Gulf War', *Journal of Strategic Studies*, 15, 3 (September 1992), p. 306.

12. Arens, *Broken Covenant*, pp. 177, 181 (see also the discussion below of the Jordanian angle).
13. *Yediot Aharonot*, 7 Days Magazine (Hebrew daily), 5 January 2001, pp. 15–20.
14. Arens, *Broken Covenant*, p. 183.
15. *Davar* (Hebrew daily), 10 August 1990, p. 1.
16. *Jerusalem Post*, 25 September 1990, p. 1.
17. *Ha'aretz* (Hebrew daily), 7 November 2000, p. A1.
18. *Maariv* (Hebrew daily), 30 December 1990, p. 1.
19. *Yediot Aharonot*, 11 January 1991, p. 2.
20. Arens, *Broken Covenant*, pp. 160–1, 164, 185–6.
21. Gerald M. Steinberg, 'Israeli Responses to the Threat of Chemical Warfare', *Armed Forces & Society*, 20, 1 (Fall 1993), pp. 85–101.
22. Arens, *Broken Covenant*, p. 168.
23. *New York Times*, 10 January 1991.
24. Asher Susser, *Jordan: Case Study of a Pivotal State*, Policy Papers, 53 (Washington, DC: Washington Institute for Near East Policy, 2000), pp. 69–90.
25. Arens, *Broken Covenant*, pp. 158–61.
26. Moshe Zak, *King Hussein Makes Peace* (Hebrew; Ramat Gan: BESA Center for Strategic Studies and Bar-Ilan University Press, 1996), pp. 35–6.
27. Shamir, *Summing-Up*, p. 265. Iraqi military presence in Jordan has traditionally been an Israeli 'red line'. See Micha Bar, *Red Lines in Israel's Deterrence Strategy* (Hebrew; Tel Aviv: Maarachot, 1990), pp. 97–9.
28. *Jerusalem Post*, 25 December 1990, p. 1.
29. For Jordanian perceptions of the situation, see Susser, *Jordan: Case Study of a Pivotal State*, pp. 72–4.
30. Zak, *King Hussein Makes Peace*, pp. 49–50.
31. Gad Barzilai, 'Israel', in *Middle East Contemporary Survey: 1990* (Boulder, CO: Westview, 1993), p. 444.
32. Baker, *The Politics of Diplomacy*, p. 385.
33. Shamir, *Summing-Up*, p. 268.
34. Arens, *Broken Covenant*, p. 178.
35. Ibid., p. 161.
36. Ibid., pp. 184–5.
37. Ibid., p. 167.
38. Ibid., pp. 168–70.
39. Ibid., p. 189.
40. Baker, *The Politics of Diplomacy*, p. 385. The third member of the American delegation was National Security Council staffer Merrill Ruck.
41. Arens, *Broken Covenant*, p. 188.
42. Ibid., p. 224.
43. Ibid., pp. 196–7.
44. Ron Ben-Yishai, 'Interview with the Chief of Staff, Lt. Gen. Ehud Barak', *Yediot Aharonot*, 29 September 1991.
45. Dan Shomron, 'Personal Report on the Gulf War', *Yediot Aharonot*, 8 September 1991.
46. David A. Welch, 'The Politics and Psychology of Restraint: Israeli Decision-Making in the Gulf War', *International Journal*, 46 (Spring 1992), p. 341.
47. Shamir, *Summing-Up*, p. 263.
48. Lawrence Freedman and Efraim Karsh, *The Gulf Conflict* (Princeton, NJ: Princeton University Press, 1993), p. 106.
49. See Shamir, *Summing-Up*, pp. 271–2; Arens, *Broken Covenant*, pp. 197–200, 208, 215–17, 229–30.
50. Arens, *Broken Covenant*, p. 206.

51. Ibid., p. 226.
52. Ibid., pp. 229–30.
53. For such a line of thinking, see Richard Ned Lebow, 'What's So Different About Counterfactual', *World Politics*, 52 (July 2000), pp. 550–85.
54. Welch, 'The Politics and Psychology of Restraint', p. 353.
55. Baker, *The Politics of Diplomacy*, p. 387.
56. Ibid.
57. Michael Gordon and Bernard Trainor, *The Generals' War* (Boston, MA: Little, Brown, 1994), p. 224.
58. Colin Powell, *My American Journey* (New York: Random House, 1995), p. 488.
59. Baker, *The Politics of Diplomacy*, p. 388.
60. Arens, *Broken Covenant*, p. 203.
61. Reuven Pedahtzur, 'The Gulf War in Israeli Eyes', *Maarachot* (Hebrew), 330 (June–July 1993), p. 14.
62. *Maariv*, 1 February 1991.
63. *Yediot Aharonot*, 19 June 1991, p. 4.
64. Arens, *Broken Covenant*, pp. 204, 212, 213.
65. Baker, *The Politics of Diplomacy*, pp. 388–9.
66. For the details, see Eisenberg, 'Passive Belligerency', pp. 314–15.
67. Baker, *The Politics of Diplomacy*, p. 390.
68. Arens, *Broken Covenant*, p. 208.
69. *Maariv*, 1 February 1991. For similar results, see *Ha'aretz*, 28 January 1991. See also Yehuda Ben-Meir, 'The Israeli Home Front in the Gulf War', in Joseph Alpher (ed.), *War in the Gulf: Implications for Israel* (Boulder, CO: Westview, 1992).
70. Gad Barzilai, 'Society and Politics in War: The Israeli Case', in Barzilai, Klieman and Shidlo, *The Gulf Crisis and Its Global Aftermath*, pp. 140–1.
71. George Simmel, *Conflict* (New York: Free Press, 1955).
72. For a convincing elaboration of this view, see Stuart Cohen in this volume.
73. For a comprehensive review of Israel's predicament in this decade, see Efraim Inbar, 'Israel's Strategic Environment of the 1990s', *Journal of Strategic Studies*, 25, 1 (March 2002).
74. For the Soviet role, see Alvin Z. Rubinstein, 'Moscow and the Gulf War: Decisions and Consequences', *International Journal*, 39 (Spring 1994), pp. 302–28.
75. Efraim Inbar, 'Arab–Israeli Coexistence: The Causes, Achievements and Limitations', *Israel Affairs*, 6, 2–3 (Spring–Summer 2000), pp. 260–1.
76. Baker, *The Politics of Diplomacy*, p. 274.
77. Ibid.
78. Shomron, 'Personal Report on the Gulf War', p. 4.
79. Zak, *King Hussein Makes Peace*, pp. 50–1.
80. Efraim Inbar and Shmuel Sandler, 'Israeli Deterrence Strategy Revisited', *Security Studies*, 3, 2 (Winter 1993/94), pp. 330–58.
81. See Shai Feldman, 'Israeli Deterrence', in Alpher, *War in the Gulf*.
82. Norman Schwartzkopf, *It Doesn't Take a Hero* (New York: Bantam Books, 1992), p. 373.
83. Baker, *The Politics of Diplomacy*, p. 385.
84. Amatzia Baram, 'Israeli Deterrence, Iraqi Responses', *Orbis*, 36, 3 (Summer 1992), pp. 398–9.
85. Thomas A. Keaney and Eliot A. Cohen, *Revolution in Warfare? Air Power in the Persian Gulf* (Annapolis, MD: Naval Institute Press, 1995), p. 72.
86. Efraim Inbar, *Rabin and Israel's National Security* (Baltimore, MD and Washington, DC: Johns Hopkins University Press and Woodrow Wilson Center Press, 1999), pp. 125, 138.

5

The (Non-)Legacy of the 1991 Gulf War: An Israeli Perspective

STUART A. COHEN

A prevalent convention of Israeli historiography is the division of the State's chronology since 1948 into individual sub-periods, marked by the country's various wars. Thus, it has become common to speak (for instance) of the 'generation' of the War of Independence; the 'period' of reprisal activities prior to the Suez War of 1956; the 'age' of the post-1967 victory; the 'years of trauma' that followed the Yom Kippur War of 1973; the 'era' of Israel's Lebanon imbroglio; and the 'experience' of the *intifada*. This war-based rhythm, which contrasts sharply with the recognition accorded to waves of immigration (*aliyot*) as units of time in the years prior to statehood, is easily explained. It reflects the extent to which Israel's modern history has been dominated by the experience of warfare, in all its various manifestations. Hence, the periodization by wars has been employed not only in military histories, but also – and with equal justification – in synoptic surveys of literature, the arts and political change. In those spheres, too, each war is said to have generated a specific genre of activity and creativity, each with its own style and agenda.

In this respect, the Gulf War of 1991 constitutes a glaring exception. Unlike almost every bout of Arab–Israeli conflict by which it was preceded and has been followed, the Gulf War did not produce any distinctive oeuvre of Israeli prose, poetry or song. At the distance of a decade, neither does it seem to have left any noticeable mark on other aspects of the country's culture or even on the course of its recent domestic political history (both of which have been influenced over the past decade far more by mass immigration, political upheaval and religious–secular dissension). Even the war's psychological impact on the personal lives of those Israelis most affected by its course seems to have been limited and of remarkably short duration.[1]

Of more particular relevance is the impression that, likewise, the Gulf War also appears to have exerted almost no independent influence of any substance on Israel's security thinking and behavior. True, this conflict did exhibit at least three novel strategic features:

- 1991 was the first year since 1948 when targets in the Israeli rear were subjected to serious attacks (on this occasion by Scud missiles rather than by aircraft).
- This was also the first time that, contrary to explicit Israeli warnings, such attacks did not elicit from the IDF an independent military response. Unusually, Israel thus became a 'passive belligerent',[2] involved in a war in which it did not fight.
- By seemingly exposing the limited value of the territorial dimension of strategic depth, the Scud missile strikes appeared to undermine what had thereto been a fundamental axiom of the country's entire security doctrine.[3]

But despite all of the above, in retrospect there nevertheless seems little justification for the snapshot deductions, initially drawn by some early commentators, that 'the war in the Gulf represents a milestone in Israel's history'.[4] Closer analysis suggests that this particular conflict did not – of itself – generate a thorough reappraisal of Israel's security culture and doctrines. The thrust of the argument of this chapter will be that quite the contrary is the case. Once the dust of conflict had settled, the course of developments in the sphere of security – as in others – appeared to follow a trajectory which in most respects had been laid down much earlier, and in others was impelled by alternative causes. In sum, the Gulf War did not cause a sudden (let alone seismic) shift in Israeli military and strategic thinking or posture. At the most, all it did was accelerate changes already under way.

In order to substantiate that argument, four distinct dimensions of the Israeli security context will be examined: (1) the possible effect of the Gulf War on Israel's identification of its principal military threats; (2) its impact on Israel's force postures; (3) its impact on Israel's force structures; and (4) the effects on the country's military–societal relations. Although in many ways convergent and mutually reinforcing, each of these four areas will be analyzed sequentially. In each category of analysis, it will here be argued, the Gulf War did not uncover anything that had not been envisioned in one form or another before its outbreak. Moreover, and even though paradigm shifts have occurred in each of those areas over the past 20 years, the contribution of the Gulf War to such developments can be said to have been – at most – only marginal. The majority of the changes that have transformed Israel's security landscape over the past decade were already in process prior to 1991. Given such extraneous phenomena as the end of the Cold War and the pace of technological–military advance in the region – as well as cultural currents within Israeli society – most of the changes that did take place would probably have occurred even had Saddam Hussein never invaded Kuwait or fired a single Scud.

IDENTIFICATION OF PRINCIPAL SECURITY THREATS

Initial official military reactions to the Scud missiles tended to play down their impact on Israel's security. Thus, in an interview given immediately after the war to the official IAF journal, the commander of the Force, Major-General Avihu Bin-Nun, altogether sought to convey a sense of confidence in the IDF's ability to deal with similar attacks in the future. After all, he emphasized, the Scuds had caused very little material damage and only a few casualties.[5] Within just four years, however, Bin-Nun's successor (Major-General Herzl Budinger) articulated in the same forum a considerably less sanguine view. The appearance of operational surface-to-surface missiles in the Middle Eastern theater, he admitted in 1995, had significantly constricted Israel's margins of security. Indeed:

The threat of surface-to-surface missiles is undoubtedly the most drastic change to have taken place in the region in recent years. ... This is probably the greatest revolution in the military sphere to have affected the state of Israel and the air force.

He later added that in a future war Israel might have to absorb as many as 200 to 400 missile attacks against targets such as Tel Aviv and Haifa.[6]

Budinger's was not only the more frank of the two opinions; it was also the more realistic reflection of changes in the IDF's overall military commitments. Clearly, the period spanned by the Gulf War did witness a restructuring of the previous hierarchy of Israel's threat perceptions.[7] The question is whether the event of the Gulf War played any significant part in this process.

Traditionally, Israeli strategic thought had been based on the assumption that the most serious security threats to the country emanated from the possibility of a cross-border invasion by neighboring conventional armies, most of which possessed virtual freedom of access to the Soviet arsenal. In Israeli strategic jargon, 'basic [military] security', i.e. the State's physical survival, fundamentally depended on the IDF's ability to deter – and if necessary to repel – massive ground attacks on Israel's perimeter, such as had seemed imminent in 1956 and 1967, and in fact took place in 1973. All other military threats were, by comparison, relegated to the realm of 'current security' concerns, a term which signified that they were considered a nuisance but not an existential danger.

'Low-intensity operations', such as were necessitated by the need to deal with occasional acts of PLO terror and insurgency in the occupied territories, constituted one obvious example of the 'current security' category. But, for several decades after 1948, so too did the defense of Israel's rear. Concern with the possibility of massive enemy attacks on Israel's civilian centers had, of course, always been present. But its impact on overall security doctrine had nevertheless been remarkably slight. Traditionally, Israeli military views of 'the next war' had always been predicated on the assumption that the IDF would be called upon to conduct swift battles of maneuver against the armies of contiguous foes. Moreover, contingency planning assumed that the fighting would principally take place on enemy territory, and would be characterized by the massive use of armored thrusts supported by tactical air strikes. In programs for both weapons acquisitions and force structures, battles of 'decision' took clear precedence over those of 'attrition',[8] and 'wars of territory' loomed larger than 'wars of [long-range] fire'. This remained the case during the early 1980s. Even then, it has been reported, 'Israeli intelligence officials and planners believed that conventional missiles in Arab arsenals were inaccurate, and therefore unlikely to cause significant damage to Israeli targets.'[9]

Clearly, the experience of the Scud attacks mandated a revision of those axioms. But, what needs to be stressed is that it was not the first to do so. In fact, the traditional order of priorities – defining which threats did affect 'basic security' and which did not – was already being questioned some time prior to 1991. In part, such revisions were necessitated by the *intifada*, which had erupted in 1987 and which soon thereafter came to constitute a major military burden, propelling to the very forefront of national consciousness concern for the personal security of individual citizens.[10] At precisely the same time (the late 1980s), former Israeli attitudes respecting the country's relative invulnerability to air and/or missile attack by a distant foe were similarly being revised. The breathing space assumed to have been won by the destruction of the Iraqi nuclear facility at Osiraq in 1981 had soon proved to be more apparent than real. True, as late as 1987, Yitzhak Rabin (then Minister of Defense) still believed that it would take another decade 'at least' for further nuclear threats to appear in the Middle East.[11] Conventional missiles, he admitted, were however another matter. By the mid-1980s, Israeli military intelligence had begun to take serious note of the progress made by both Syria and Iraq in missile technology, production and deployment.[12] Moreover, as early as the summer of 1986, Rabin was explicitly warning the public of the possibility that surface-to-surface missiles might land on Israeli population centers in a future Arab–Israeli military encounter, and thereby entirely revolutionize Israeli experiences of the character of war.[13]

94

The 'war of the cities' fought by Iran and Iraq in the early spring of 1988, when each side bombarded the capital city of the other with missiles, provided an immediate and graphic example of the sort of scenario which Rabin presumably had in mind. It also served to shift the geographical locus of Israeli military attention. Thereto, most official Israeli discussions of the likelihood of conventional missile attacks had been predicated on the assumption that they would emanate from Syria (as in fact had already been the case in 1973).[14] As early as 1988, however, Iraq and – increasingly – Iran were becoming identified as equally likely sources.[15] By the time of the second Gulf War, some of the doctrinal obligations were being publicly aired.[16]

Just as the Gulf War cannot be held responsible for the genesis of the realignment in Israel's threat perceptions over the past two decades, so too neither can it be considered responsible for the subsequent strength of the new order of its priorities. Undoubtedly, the Scud attacks of 1991 did add a sense of urgency to the need to define Israel's security concerns anew. Nevertheless, to attribute the post-Gulf refinements in Israel's threat perceptions entirely (or even mainly) to the events of that year is, it seems, to oversimplify what was in fact a far more complex process. Even as catalysts, far more decisive was the cumulative influence exerted in the immediately following years by a disparate cluster of other transformations in Israel's regional and global strategic environment. Within this latter category come, especially, the intensification of perceptions of the danger posed by Iran, at both a non-conventional and sub-conventional level; the growing eclipse of Soviet/Russian influence in the region; and – on another plane – Rabin's narrow victory in the 1992 elections.

In retrospect, there can be little doubt that these were the developments that set in motion the processes that eventually resulted in the attempts to reach an accommodation with Syria, the new departure in Israeli–Palestinian relations signified by the 1993 Oslo agreement, and (far more successfully) the 1994 Aravah treaty with Jordan. Whilst it would be inappropriate to present here detailed analyses of the train of events that led to each of these steps, the conclusions of the available studies do warrant attention. All emphasize two major points. One is the importance of Rabin's electoral victory to these expressions of Israel's strategic realignment (notwithstanding the Gulf War, it is highly unlikely that his predecessor, Yitzhak Shamir, would have been prepared to sanction similar moves). The other is the wide spectrum of influences responsible for generating the shift in Rabin's own thinking. Of these, the most important were: his conviction that the implosion of the Soviet Union presented Israel with 'a window of strategic opportunity' that had to be exploited by bringing Syria to the negotiating table; his growing sensitivity to the threat presented by Iran – in view of both the latter's growing nuclear potential and sponsorship of Islamic fundamentalism; and his appreciation of the decline in the threshold of the Israeli public's tolerance to sustain casualties (whether they be caused by conventional warfare or terrorist attacks).[17] By comparison, the Gulf War *per se* exerted only a marginal impact.

FORCE POSTURES

As several analysts have noted, the redefinition of Israel's principal security threats over the past two decades has also necessitated a parallel shift in its force postures. Admittedly, the changes in this sphere have been somewhat less blatant and hence considerably less amenable to synoptic description. One principal reason for the relative obscurity surrounding this subject is the reluctance of the members of Israel's own security community to formulate anything like a coherent statement of strategic doctrine. Altogether, the Israeli 'style' in matters of strategic conceptualization has always been brazenly unsystematic. Its National Security Council (itself a fledgling body that still lacks any real influence) has yet to formulate a written version of an integrated national security doctrine. Similarly, and as Israel's State Comptroller had occasion to remark in September 2000, neither has the IDF itself ever published comprehensive and 'official' manuals of force missions, let alone subjected them to regular and systematic review.[18] Most of the fundamental notions that have dominated Israel's strategic discourse for almost half a century have invariably been treated as axioms to be revered rather than as propositions deserving of periodic critical examination.

It has always been taken for granted, for instance, that Israel's preferred force posture is one of deterrence, primarily conventional but in the last resort of a nuclear variety, too. Should deterrence fail, it has similarly been assumed the IDF would seek to fight an offensive (and if possible pre-emptive) 'short war', characterized by the deployment of conventional forces in high-tempo battles of maneuver, preferably on enemy territory.[19] Above all, the prevalent thinking has always been that Israel would have to fight its battles alone. Hence, although the history of Israeli statecraft is replete with examples of a search for at least one ally amongst the great powers,[20] such efforts were never allowed to undermine the priority of 'self-reliance' in Israel's underlying strategic posture.

Formally, each of those principles still holds. Indeed, to read available expositions of current Israeli security thinking (all necessarily 'unofficial' in nature) is to gain a rather monotonous impression of entrenched strategic diagnosis and repetitive military prognosis. Very much like their predecessors, the latest versions too stress the need for Israel to seek self-sufficiency in as many spheres of defense as possible – a principle which explains both the retention of Israel's traditionally 'opaque' nuclear policy as well as its heavy investments in advanced home-grown conventional capabilities. True, the disdain with which Saddam Hussein ignored repeated Israeli warnings to refrain from missile strikes in 1991 did – eventually – give rise to concerns in some academic circles about an erosion of the IDF's deterrent capacity.[21] Nevertheless, as far as the military is concerned, the retention of a basic deterrent posture remains an article of faith.[22] So too does the preferred operational mode should deterrence fail. Here, too, most contemporary analysts seem simply to echo the conventional wisdom of an earlier generation. Specifically, they advocate that in a future war the IDF must seek to repeat its earlier successes (notably that of 1967) by striking swiftly and hard, aiming at the decisive destruction of Arab forces, conventional and irregular alike, *in situ*.[23]

This cluster of guiding principles not only accounts for the aura of continuity that surrounds the tenor of Israeli declarations of military intent. In a more material sense, those principles also seem to provide justification for several important strands of the IDF's recent armaments policies, and in particular those designed to augment the military's ability to attack (or to threaten to attack) targets located at considerable distances from its own bases. This, of course, is not at all a novel aspiration. Indeed, Israel demonstrated its long-range strike capabilities as early as July 1976, when launching the rescue mission at Entebbe (a distance of 3,800 kilometers), and provided further examples by destroying the Iraqi nuclear installation at Osiraq (1,500 kilometers) in June 1981 and the PLO headquarters in Tunis (2,500 kilometers) in 1988. During the 1990s, its determination to retain that capacity was sustained. One testimony is provided by the decision (finally approved in February 1993, but tabled by the IAF several years earlier) to acquire a fleet of F-15I fighter aircraft, rather than the cheaper F-16s, a decision explicitly justified by the fact that the F-15s can carry a heavier payload over greater distances in all weathers. Even more interesting has been the concurrent interest in acquiring an entirely new sea-based long-range strike potential, exemplified by the decision (again, taken as long ago as 1989) to acquire two Dolphin-class submarines capable of launching non-conventional as well as conventional missiles.[24]

Notwithstanding these signs of continuity in Israel's strategic postures, at least two fundamental changes in their basic contours can nevertheless be observed. One, analyzed by Efraim Inbar, is a tentative willingness to test the possibility of supplementing the old insistence on self-reliance by experiments in a form of collaborative security, or even security regimes.[25] The other, most recently noted by Dore Gold, Israel's Ambassador to the UN between 1997 and 1999, is a more pronounced inclination to adopt a policy of deterrence by denial, in preference to Israel's traditional emphasis on deterrence by punishment. The implication of the first of these two shifts is that Israel will in the future increasingly seek to work within multi-national frameworks in pursuit of its security aims – notwithstanding the restraints which those frameworks might necessarily place on its own long-cherished freedom of independent action. The implication of the second shift is still more substantial, not least in terms of operational contingencies. It indicates that, in a future war, the IDF might abandon its previous predilection for offensive operations and instead adopt a mode that is essentially defensive in nature.[26] To be more specific, in the event of hostilities being thought inevitable, no longer would the IDF seek to pre-empt an enemy offensive by initiating a strike of its own (the strategy adopted in 1956, in 1967 and – on a more limited scale – in the Osiraq raid of 1981). Even if themselves subjected to attack, neither would Israeli forces necessarily seek to move as quickly as possible on to a counter-offensive (as was the case in 1973). Instead, the IDF would seek to absorb the blows over an extended period, always seeking to minimize the material and human damage that they are bound to cause.

The influence of the Gulf War on the first of these shifts, away from a policy of self-reliance and towards one of what might be termed 'burden sharing', cannot be denied. As has long been recognized, that experience did undoubtedly show the Israelis – and others – the existence of clear limits to their traditional search for autonomy or limited independence (a lesson already made clearly apparent, in Israel's case, by the need to cancel the Lavi jetfighter project in 1987). At the same time, however, the 1991 conflict also demonstrated the extent to which Israel could rely on external military aid in case of real need. As much was seemingly proved both by the scale of General Schwarzkopf's investment of coalition resources in attempts to seek and destroy Iraq's Scud launchers, and by the alacrity with which the Bush administration dispatched US crews to man some of the Patriot batteries stationed in Israel during the course of the conflict. Both events helped to ease what was in many other respects a particularly tense phase of the Bush–Shamir relationship.[27] To a degree, they also prompted subsequent Israeli governments to make provisions for more wide-ranging multi-national security arrangements in other contingencies.

Although tentative, and always cautious, that process was nevertheless undeniable. After the Gulf War, Israel undertook a series of moves which indicated a clear shift towards what Inbar has termed 'a revised security paradigm'.[28] No Israeli leaders were prepared to entrust the country's entire security to others. But several did now argue that self-reliance had become less feasible, and hence proclaimed the advantages of security-related multilateral collaboration. This, certainly, became a principal plank in Rabin's thinking, and one that reflected his growing conviction that new realities warranted an abandonment of the 'ghetto mentality' by which Israeli strategic thinking had for so long been characterized. Thus, in presenting his new cabinet to the Knesset on 13 July 1992, Rabin explicitly emphasized that 'Israel is no longer "a people that dwells alone" ... and has to join the global journey towards peace, reconciliation and international cooperation.' In a speech delivered the following year to the graduates of Israel's National Security College he was equally forthright:

> The world is *no longer* against us ... states which never stretched out their hand to us, states which condemned us, which fought us, which assisted our bitterest enemies ... regard us today as a worthy and respectable address ... This is a new reality ... We must think differently ... Peace requires a world of new concepts.[29]

The moves in that direction can be clearly documented. They were not restricted merely to signing, for the very first time, international arms control and/or limitation treaties.[30] More frequently than ever before, Israel now also attempted to enlist international support in what it termed 'the global struggle against Islamic fundamentalist world-wide terrorism'.[31] At a more immediately practical level, it also evinced a greater readiness than ever to commit some of its own immediate security needs to international care. One striking example is provided by Rabin's agreement to the establishment of a Temporary International Presence in Hebron (TIPH) in February 1994. Another can be seen in his willingness to consider stationing US troops on the Golan (as monitors) in case of an Israel–Syria peace treaty.[32] Yet a third is Ehud Barak's agreement to the stationing of UN forces along the Israeli–Lebanese border after the IDF withdrawal in May 2000.

But with respect to the second shift in Israeli security postures, to a reliance on deterrence by denial rather than on deterrence by punishment, the influence of the Gulf War seems to have been far less clear cut. True, several analyses published in the immediate aftermath of the conflict did loudly proclaim the need for Israel to adopt a more defensive strategy against future missile attacks, arguing that the events of 1991 had altogether exposed the futility of the old offensive posture of deterrence by punishment. In Ze'ev Schiff's words:

> As soon as the Iraqi missiles began landing on Israel, it became obvious that the country's long-standing security doctrine – requiring that as soon as the war breaks out, the Israel Defense Force (IDF) must shift the fighting onto the enemy's territory – had become outdated. [33]

But closer scrutiny reveals that this was by no means an altogether novel message. Calls for Israel to reassess its old security strategies in favor of a new mode had in fact been voiced several years before the Gulf War.[34] More to the point, official Israeli interest in the acquisition of an independent and extended anti-missile umbrella similarly predated that conflict. Indeed, the wisdom (financial as well as operational) of this course, as an alternative to either pre-emption or retaliation, had been hotly debated inside and outside the military establishment throughout the second half of the 1980s.[35] Although the issue does not seem to have been settled (at least in Rabin's mind) until the Iran–Iraq 'war of the cities' towards the end of the decade, the drive to acquire some form of missile shield had immediately thereafter already begun to gather momentum.

The milestones on this particular road can be briefly summarized. The first of any practical significance occurred in 1987, when Israel jumped at President Reagan's invitation to participate in the Strategic Defense Initiative (SDI) program, thus becoming the first foreign country to do so. Two years thereafter, and with considerable American financial backing, Israel also began to develop its own program (significantly code-named *Homah*, which translates as 'Wall'), whose linchpin was an anti-missile missile, eventually to be known as the Arrow. As an interim measure (and, again, before the invasion of Kuwait) Israel had in 1989 also begun negotiations to purchase the PAC-2 version of the Patriot surface-to-air missile which, although essentially an anti-aircraft weapon, had – so its manufacturers claimed – also demonstrated some anti-missile potential.[36] Meanwhile, and as part of the same effort, Israel in September 1988 launched its first independent high-resolution reconnaissance satellite (Ofek-1; Ofek-2 followed in April 1990). During the same period, it also began to bolster the country's passive defenses. Specifically, it was in the late 1980s that the IDF began the process of investigation and analysis which was, in 1990, to result in the decision to establish an entirely new Rear Command.

Undeniably, the experience of the Gulf War did (again) inject a sense of urgency into many of such efforts. This was most obviously true in the area of civil defense preparations, the inadequacies of which were fully exposed during the Gulf War and which soon thereafter became the subject of a stringent investigation by the State Comptroller (much of which still remains classified).[37] Space-based intelligence similarly received augmented attention after 1991, not least in view of Israel's embarrassingly obvious dependence during the Gulf hostilities on the early warning of an impending attack provided by American facilities.[38] At the same time, efforts were made to cooperate with the Americans in developing a Boost Phase Intercept (BPI) project, as a supplement to the Arrow.[39]

But the lines of cause and effect between the Gulf War and other manifestations of post-1991 Israeli efforts to attain a missile defense system are far more tenuous. The fact that significant advances were undoubtedly made towards reaching that goal over the next decade[40] does not itself prove very much. All it indicates is that the momentum generated before 1991 was thereafter maintained, and even then probably more due to the growing realization of the threat posed by Iran than as a result of any specific analysis of the experience of the Scud attacks. Hence, to attribute the pace of the Arrow's development, for instance, entirely – or even principally – to the Gulf War is, once again, to overlook the true genealogy both of that specific program and of the state of mind that gave it birth. As has been pointed out, recent changes in the IDF's military doctrines cannot be attributed to any specific event. They result, rather, from incremental transformations in the entire spectrum of Israel's technological, diplomatic and societal strategic environment. It is these that explain why 'Israel's war objectives are assuming a more "negative" character, aimed first and foremost at denying the enemy any military or political achievements' rather than bringing him to defeat on the battlefield.[41]

FORCE STRUCTURES

The decade since 1991 has certainly witnessed reforms in Israel's military force structures that in some cases warrant depiction as revolutionary. Baldly summarized, those reforms have taken three main forms:

- The first, and most obvious, relates to the **composition** of the IDF. As observers have been pointing out for some years now, the Force has slowly and unofficially (but nevertheless surely and perhaps irreversibly) relinquished several of its traditional attributes as a 'people's army'. One striking manifestation of this development has been the extent to which conscription – for men as well as women – has gradually become more selective, thereby undermining the traditional view of military service as a rite of passage towards full citizenship and an all-encompassing enunciation of national identity. So large is the number of 18-year-olds now being altogether excused from conscription, and so frequent the issue of early discharges to those who are drafted, that a full three years of duty is well on the way to becoming the exception rather than the norm. With regard to the reserves, the differentials have become even more stark. Once a ubiquitous feature of many an Israeli's private life, reserve service is now very much a minority phenomenon. As long ago as 1996, the Head of IDF Human Resources Division, General Gideon Sheffer, admitted that only 25 per cent of listed reservists aged 21 to 51 actually performed any service at all, and that 90 per cent of those who did so were under 39 years of age.[42]

- In tandem, and partly in consequence, the past decade has also witnessed a transformation in the **ethos** of the Force. Briefly, this can be categorized as a clear movement towards what Professor Charles Moskos has termed an 'occupational' attitude towards service. Evident at the level of both conscripts and reserves (where those who do complete their full terms of service are now entitled to cash awards and post-service financial benefits), this characteristic has become particularly pronounced amongst the professional segment of the Force. Long gone (if they ever truly existed) are the days when talented conscripts on the eve of discharge could be expected to 'sign on' for extended terms of professional service simply in response to the call of national necessity. Gone, too, however, are the days when the IDF was itself prepared to offer tenure (with the promise of retirement on full pension at the age of 45) to virtually anyone who expressed a wish to enlist as a military professional. Matters are now much more complex. Personnel whose retention is deemed 'essential' to the maintenance of the IDF's qualitative combat edge are being offered an increasingly attractive package of educational, housing and salary benefits.[43] At the same time, however, 'non-essential' professionals, many of whose medical, construction and food services are being progressively outsourced to civilian contractors, are being steadily discharged.

- Equally striking, thirdly, are signs of **organizational changes** within the IDF. At their most basic, these take the form of attempts to apply technological innovations to administrative staff work, not least by introducing computerized systems of accountancy and management at all levels of command. But they also take at least two more substantive forms. One is the greater emphasis on the training in the ability to exploit new information- and knowledge-based systems of command, control and surveillance throughout the combat and combat-support services. The other – and still more far-reaching – has been the initiation of a series of fundamental changes into the IDF's entire hierarchy. These range from the inauguration in November 1997 of *Aviv Neurim* ('Spring Youth'), a program designed to 'flatten' the military structure by granting greater managerial and budgetary autonomy to middle-range commands,[44] to the establishment early in 1999 of the Ground Arms Command, a framework that endows the IDF's combined land forces with the status of an independent arm.[45]

It is tempting to attribute many components of this cluster of changes, too, to the influence exerted by the Gulf War. This is so especially since the IDF – like all other Western armies – did undoubtedly take to heart the evidence provided by Desert Storm of the potential inherent in the 'Revolution in Military Affairs' (indeed, perhaps more so since it was not a participant in Desert Storm and hence could only learn its lessons from observation).[46] This argument was widely reiterated by Ehud Barak (the IDF's Vice-Chief of Staff during the Gulf War and Chief of Staff 1991–94), whose frequent public pronouncements on military affairs were in the wake of Desert Storm liberally laced with references to 'the future battlefield' and its demands. Other members of the General Staff imparted the same message. The Gulf War, they argued, showed that:

> [t]he wars of the future [would similarly] be saturated with fire. The importance of the concentration of weapons' power will be paramount. The accuracy and long-range precision of battle platforms will initiate us into a new era … [i]n which technology will be more important than mass and the quality of soldiers more important than their numbers. Qualitative weapons in the hands of mediocre operators is no panacea for military problems.[47]

In this area, too, however, initial impressions are misleading. Once again, closer scrutiny of the chronological record reveals that the pressure to undertake reforms in Israel's military structure in fact antedated the Gulf War by several years. What is more, the same record also suggests that the pace of post-1991 developments in these fields likewise owed comparatively little to the stimulus provided by the demonstration of the superiority of the US order of battle during Desert Storm. The reforms in the IDF's force structure, undertaken during the 1990s, owed far less to a wish to emulate American achievements against Iraq[48] than to the pressure of an entire spectrum of alternative events.

First, the historical record. Israeli force planners have always been receptive to the notion that they have to maintain a qualitative edge over their potential enemies, as much in organizational as in technological terms, in order to compensate for the IDF's inherent numerical inferiority.[49] By the 1980s, the need for the IDF to adapt both its structure and its complement to changes in Israel's technological–strategic environment had become especially acute. As a result, as early as 1983, the IDF had announced the establishment of a Ground Forces Command, which in many respects can be seen as the precursor of today's Ground Arms Command. More substantially, in 1987 the Knesset's Foreign Affairs and Defense Committee established a special secret subcommittee (the Meridor Committee) to study the influence of technological and strategic changes on Israel's force structures and produce a specific checklist of required responses.[50] Within a year, Chief of Staff Dan Shomron had begun to popularize one of the Committee's principal conclusions, when proclaiming the need for what he termed 'a smaller and smarter' Force. With the ground thus prepared, all Barak had to do was make detailed recommendations (a task that he delegated to the Shaffir Committee, established in 1992 with a mandate to study manpower reforms in specific detail) and lay down a timetable for their implementation. It seems fair to assume that he would have undertaken this step even had the Gulf War never occurred.[51]

The pace of subsequent progress in this area leads to a similar conclusion with respect to the following decade. Notwithstanding the encouragement that the Gulf War undoubtedly provided to supporters of a smaller and smarter IDF, progress towards attaining that goal was, until the very end of the 1990s, noticeably slow and piecemeal. Whether this was because of sheer bureaucratic inertia, increasing budgetary constraints[52] or the short-term requirements of the Lebanon campaign – which, either singly or in combination, are the three principal candidates for blame – is really beside the point. More relevant is the fact that the accelerator for change provided by the Gulf War was insufficient in itself to overcome those brakes.

It is even doubtful whether the Gulf War deserves to be numbered amongst the specific events that did most influence the pace of whatever progress towards IDF structural reform has become apparent in the past few years. In retrospect, two other trends – both much broader in scope – can be said to have exerted a far greater impact. The first, both chronologically and in order of importance, was the feeling in military circles that diplomatic developments (specifically, Israel's peace treaties with Egypt and Jordan and its strategic partnership with Turkey) were so conducive to reducing the dangers once posed by Israel's contiguous neighbors that the IDF was now able to concentrate on building an army best tailored to deal with its long-range foes.[53] The other was the appreciation that developments of a cultural nature within Israel's domestic society were in any case undermining the resilience of the IDF's traditional structure, and indeed calling into question its very *raison d'être*. The first of those developments has already been itemized. It is to the second that attention must now be turned.

MILITARY–SOCIETAL RELATIONS

Of all the transformations that have taken place in Israel's overall strategic environment over the past two decades, the decline in the centrality of the IDF in the cultural consciousness of Israeli society at large constitutes by far the most dramatic – and may even be the most portentous. Such, certainly, is the impression conveyed by the attention now being accorded to the subject in discussions of grand strategy at various levels of high command.[54] Still more indicative of concern is the tone that permeates senior military references to the topic, which in some cases approaches the apocalyptic. A renowned example occurred in October 1996, when Chief of the IDF General Staff,

Major-General Amnon Lipkin-Shahak, delivered an emotional eulogy on the first anniversary of Prime Minister Yitzhak Rabin's assassination:

> The ties binding the IDF and civilian society – which once constituted the very soul of the army, part of its uniqueness and a source of its strength – have now become burdensome ...
>
> How far we are, O captain, from the days when a military uniform was a source of pride and self-respect. During the past year, as a result of a process which commenced long ago but which has gained momentum [we have seen] soldiers and officers, conscripts, professionals and reservists, walking around in our midst with an almost apologetic look on their faces ...
>
> Definitions alter, values are replaced, and as if subject to the whims of computerized graphics, the Israeli changes his demeanor and society revises its form. Non-service ... no longer constitutes a stigma, and voluntarism, the act of giving out of a wish to contribute, no longer receives the respect it deserves.[55]

When placed in historical perspective, the grounds for that judgement are easily apparent. Throughout the first quarter-century of its history, the IDF basked in a climate of virtually totemistic domestic esteem. Public support for the Force constituted an essential and integral ingredient of what has been called Israel's 'civil religion'.[56] Moreover, military service was broadly recognized to be the primary expression of citizen fulfillment. Under those circumstances, the IDF had no cause to fear that civilian agencies (whether governmental or non-governmental) might intrude into professional spheres of military activity. The principle of military subordination to political direction was, of course, widely touted and deeply ingrained. Moreover, public interest in all aspects of military behavior was high – and, indeed, deliberately cultivated by the official orchestration of an entire panoply of activities that, together, created an atmosphere of almost blatant 'cultural militarism'.[57] But within those confines, the IDF enjoyed a degree of corporate autonomy that extended to the very limits of democratic acceptability. Other spheres of government – education, social welfare, international alignment, immigration and religious legislation – were publicly scrutinized with a degree of intensity that was sometimes inquisitorial. A cocoon of reverence that invariably precluded any form of public inspection whatsoever, however, protected military affairs. By the same token, generals (in and out of uniform) were invested with a quasi-mythological stature and thus all but placed beyond the reach of conventional public accountability.

As analysts have been pointing out for over a decade, those conditions no longer apply.[58] Indeed, they began to change as early as 1973, when the IDF first swayed on its pedestal of infallibility. True, even thereafter military influence on all spheres of public life remained uncommonly high (as is still well illustrated by the number of retired generals who continue to affect a lateral transfer into politics or local government). But in other respects overall Israeli public attitudes towards the IDF and its commanders have clearly undergone paradigm shifts over the past 25 years.[59] One expression of the change can be discerned in the increasing extent to which the media, the courts and – not least – organized groups of parents have begun to cast off their previous bounds of self-imposed restraint and now subject the military and its operations to an increasing degree of critical scrutiny. A second is to be found in fluctuations in the degree of motivation to military service amongst conscripts and – still more markedly – amongst reservists.

No less interesting than the signs indicative of a sea-change in societal attitudes to the military is the evidence of the IDF's response. Sensitive to the prevailing atmosphere, senior military staff have found it politic to take measures deliberately designed to defuse potential mines of military–societal tension. Thus, the Force has adopted a noticeably more deferential attitude towards the press and the civilian judicial system. It has also introduced a more user-friendly system of conscription assignments that takes into account the wishes of the individual new recruit, and instructed Force commanders to allocate a larger proportion of their time to maintaining contact with the families of the troops in their charge. Amongst the many other steps that the IDF has taken in an attempt to bring itself into line with public expectations, particularly noteworthy are the publication of an 'Ethical Code',[60] a new-found emphasis on gender integration and on the reduction of sexual harassment in the ranks and (as has already been noted) a readiness to offer specifically material rewards for military service.

How much did the experience of the Gulf War contribute to this multifaceted process? The short answer must surely be 'not very much at all'. Undeniably, the flight from Tel Aviv of some residents at the height of the 1991 Scud attacks[61] did arouse concern in senior defense circles with respect to the Israeli public's staying power. Thereafter, military references to the apparently low threshold of the civilian ability to sustain punishment became steadily more insistent.[62] But not even that record allows of the conclusion that the Gulf War deserves to be considered a turning-point in the overall balance of relations between the IDF and Israeli society at large. Overwhelmingly, the remainder of the evidence points in the opposite direction. Of themselves, the events of 1991 did not suddenly generate military fears that society was caving in. Neither, to take the other side of the societal–military coin, did they bring about an equally immediate collapse of civilian confidence in the IDF's ability to fulfill its role as the nation's primary line of defense. In both respects, the trajectory of developments was far more complex.

Take, first of all, military perceptions of society. The flight from Tel Aviv in 1991, it is worth remembering, was not the first phenomenon of its kind. As several commentators acknowledged at the time, it had clearly been portended by the reactions of many residents of the Galilee to the experience of Katyusha attacks almost exactly a decade earlier.[63] What is more, the rising incidence of conscientious objection (sometimes blatant, but more often 'gray', conscientious objection) to military service during both the Lebanon War of 1982–85 and the *intifada* had likewise indicated the extent to which restraints of a societal nature might limit the IDF's freedom of action.[64] From that perspective, the experience of the Gulf War added little that was new. It merely confirmed the existence of a process that had long been evident – and that was to resurface at such subsequent moments of tension as occurred in January and December of 1998, when the fear of a renewed missile strike by Iraq was rife.[65] It was only the cumulative impact exerted by such repeated demonstrations of public weakness that (very belatedly) led some members of the General Staff to consider their operational implications.[66] In the short term, the Gulf War gave rise to no such lessons.

A closer look at public perceptions of the IDF leads to a similar conclusion. With the massive – but unique – exception of one lengthy newspaper article (and that by a relatively obscure professor of Hebrew literature),[67] public comment throughout the Gulf War was uniformly supportive both of government policy and of the military posture of restraint that was its consequence. In this respect, the Gulf War must clearly be distinguished from both the Yom Kippur War of 1973 and the first Lebanon campaign of 1982, when outright public criticism of operations had been rife. Moreover, whereas those two previous experiences had caused some wavering of the public's confidence in the IDF, the Gulf War seemed to show that the military authorities were the only reliable source of guidance and information. That was certainly the dominant public impression once the IDF spokesman, Mr Nachman Shai, assumed the role of 'national comforter' and began to broadcast authoritative-sounding instructions before and after each and every Scud attack.[68]

Polls of public opinion seem to confirm that conclusion. Detailed surveys conducted by Gad Barzilai and Efraim Inbar between 1988 and 1994 clearly demonstrated that the Gulf War exerted no significant influence on Israeli public opinion with regards to the use of force.[69] Its effect on public confidence in the military's ability to defend Israel's security was similarly marginal, and at the time vastly overshadowed by the more lasting impact of the *intifada*.[70] Asher Arian's findings were not very different. Although 29 per cent of his respondents said that the Gulf War had changed their opinions regarding the security and political situation, the remaining 71 per cent denied that it had done so. Together with other evidence, this led to the conclusion that this particular conflict (unlike others) did not revolutionize Israeli public opinion. Rather, it 'underscored the basic features of the Israeli political system in the early 1990s, and even reinforced them'.[71]

The conclusion, it seems, is self-evident. Since 1991, the Israeli public has certainly demonstrated both increasing 'war weariness' and a progressively lower regard for most things military.[72] But there exists no substance to the hypothesis that such trends might be linked to the events of that year. Any such correlation is more apparent than real. Altogether, it has been suggested, 'in democracies, tendencies in public opinion are … influenced by domestic characteristics rather than by outside stimuli'.[73] Such certainly seems to have been the case regarding Israeli society's attitudes towards the IDF. To seek the principal causes for the faster tempo of change in this sphere in the experience of any particular episode of conflict is, it seems, to look in the wrong place. What determined how those episodes were perceived and understood was, rather, more deep-seated cultural factors – of which a growing shift towards a local version of 'postmodernism' is undoubtedly the most influential. This, it is here argued, would have occurred even had the Gulf War never taken place.

CONCLUSIONS

Necessarily, perceptions of the Gulf War have changed over time. Focusing on its impact on overall Israeli security thinking, this chapter has attempted to place that conflict in historical context, by looking at both what happened before and what happened afterwards. From neither perspective, it has here been argued, does the Gulf War deserve to be considered a watershed. Over the past decade, several aspects of Israeli strategic thinking and behavior have certainly undergone significant transformations. So much is this so that it has become appropriate to speak of a 'new' Israeli security environment that in many respects is virtually the converse of the 'old'. But to attribute most (or even many) of those changes to the war itself is, it seems, to overemphasize its impact and thus to misconstrue the record. Closer analysis reveals, rather, that the changes reflected the influence of a far wider spectrum of antecedent and subsequent circumstances, whose individual links with the Gulf War are tenuous in the extreme. Hence, our audit of the impact of war has produced almost entirely negative results. The more the events of 1991 recede inexorably into history, the more apparent it becomes that they served merely as catalysts in an elongated process. Most of the structural and intellectual vulnerabilities in Israel's strategic thought and practice then underscored had already been exposed before Iraq launched the Scud missiles. Others were not to become apparent until several years later, by which time the memory of those attacks had patently begun to fade.

NOTES

1. Zahava Solomon, *Coping with War-Induced Stress: The Gulf War and the Israeli Response* (New York: Plenum Press, 1995), p. 54.
2. Laura Zittrain Eisenberg, 'Passive Belligerency: Israel and the 1991 Gulf War', *Journal of Strategic Studies*, 15, 3 (September 1992), pp. 304–29.
3. Reuven Pedahtzur, 'The Gulf War – An Initial Critical Analysis', *Maarachot* (Hebrew), 321 (June 1991), pp. 6–14; Shimon Peres, 'Peace is Strategic Depth', in Natan Shaham and Zvi Ra'anan (eds), *War in the Gulf* (Hebrew; Tel Aviv: Sifriyat Poalim, 1991), pp. 23–31.
4. Y. Ben-Meir, 'The Israeli Home Front in the Gulf War', in Joseph Alpher (ed.), *War in the Gulf: Implications for Israel* (Tel Aviv: Jaffee Center for Strategic Studies, 1992), p. 327. 'Watershed' was the term used by Reuven Pedahtzur, 'The Gulf War in Israeli Eyes', *Maarachot* (Hebrew), 330 (June 1993), pp. 5–17.
5. *Bitaon Cheil Ha'avir* (Hebrew), 81 (October 1991), p. 3.
6. Ibid., 103 (June 1995), p. 6.
7. Stuart A. Cohen, 'Israel's Changing Military Commitments, 1981–1991: Causes and Consequences', *Journal of Strategic Studies*, 15, 3 (September 1992), pp. 330–50.
8. Stuart A. Cohen and Efraim Inbar, 'A Taxonomy of Israel's Use of Force', *Comparative Strategy*, 10 (April 1991), pp. 121–38.
9. Marvin Feuerwerger, *The Arrow Next Time? Israel's Missile Defense Program for the 1990s*, Policy Papers No. 28 (Washington, DC: Washington Institute for Near East Policy, 1991), p. 4.
10. On the *intifada* as a military burden: Efraim Inbar, 'Israel's Small War: The Military Reaction to the Intifada', *Armed Forces & Society*, 18 (Fall 1991), pp. 29–50. See also Stuart A. Cohen, 'How Did the Intifada Affect the IDF?', *Conflict Quarterly*, 14 (1994), pp. 7–22.
11. Cited in Efraim Inbar, *Rabin and Israel's National Security* (Baltimore, MD and Washington, DC: Johns Hopkins University Press and Woodrow Wilson Center Press, 1999), p. 123.
12. Feuerwerger, *The Arrow Next Time*, p. 5.
13. Inbar, *Rabin and Israel's National Security*, p. 124.
14. For retrospective evidence of Israeli concern with respect to Syrian missile development during the 1980s, see David Ivri and Ariel Levite, 'Ground to Ground Tactical Ballistic Missiles – The Threat and the Response from an Israeli Perspective', *Maarachot* (Hebrew), 356–7 (March 1998), pp. 5–11.
15. Yitzhak Rabin, 'Quality that will Guarantee Strength', in Ze'ev Tzur (ed.), *Israel's Security in the Next Decade* (Hebrew; Efal: Yad Tabenkin, 1988), pp. 39–40; and interview with Rabin in *Ha'aretz* (Hebrew daily), New Year Supplement, 29 September 1989, p. B2.
16. Uzi Rubin, 'How to Defend Against Ballistic Missiles', *Maarachot* (Hebrew), 321 (June 1991), pp. 30–5. The editor's note specifically remarks that the article was

written prior to the Gulf War.

17. See Jane Corbin, *Gaza First: The Secret Norway Channel to Peace Between Israel and the PLO* (London: Bloomsbury, 1994); Moshe Ma'oz, *Syria and Israel: From War to Peacemaking* (Oxford: Clarendon Press, 1995), esp. pp. 204–25; Itamar Rabinovitch, *The Edge of Peace: Israel and Syria, 1992–1996* (Hebrew; Tel Aviv: Yediot Aharonot, 1998); Moshe Zak, *King Hussein Makes Peace* (Hebrew; Ramat Gan: BESA Center for Strategic Studies and Bar-Ilan University Press, 1996).

18. Israel State Comptroller, *Annual Report*, No. 51a (Hebrew; Jerusalem: Government Printing House, September 2000), pp. 108–13.

19. Dan Horowitz, 'The Israeli Concept of National Security', in Avner Yaniv (ed.), *National Security and Democracy in Israel* (Boulder, CO: Lynne Rienner, 1993), pp. 11–53; and Michael I. Handel, 'The Evolution of Israeli Strategy: The Psychology of Insecurity and the Quest for Absolute Security', in Williamson Murray, MacGregor Knox and Alvin Bernstein (eds), *The Making of Strategy: Rulers, States and War* (Cambridge: Cambridge University Press, 1995), pp. 534–78.

20. See Uri Bialer, *Between East and West* (Cambridge: Cambridge University Press, 1990).

21. Much of the conventional wisdom still maintains that, the Scud attacks notwithstanding, Israeli deterrence had sufficed to prevent Saddam launching chemical attacks, e.g. Ze'ev Schiff, 'Israeli Deterrence', in Alpher, *War in the Gulf*, pp. 170–89; Ze'ev Schiff, 'Israel After the War', *Foreign Affairs*, 70, 2 (Spring 1991), pp. 25–9; Gabriel Ben-Dor, 'Arab Rationality and Deterrence', in A. Klieman (ed.), *Deterrence in the Middle East* (Tel Aviv: Jaffee Center for Strategic Studies, 1993), pp. 87–97. That view has, however, been strenuously challenged in Efraim Inbar and Shmuel Sandler, 'Israel's Deterrence Strategy Revisited', *Security Studies*, 3 (Winter 1993/94), pp. 330–58.

22. Gen. (ret.) Ilan Biran, 'Our Secret Weapon – Deterrence', *Shiryon* (Hebrew; official journal of IDF Armored Corps), 6 (October 1999), pp. 42–3.

23. Israel Tal, *National Security: The Israeli Experience* (Westport, CT: Praeger, 2000), pp. 45–76.

24. The last of the pair of submarines (built in Germany) was delivered in the summer of 2000. On the implications for Israeli strike-power see Ze'ev Schiff, 'An Opening for a New Strategy', *Ha'aretz*, 31 May 2000, p. B1.

25. Efraim Inbar, 'Israel: The Shift from Self-Reliance', in Benjamin Frankel (ed.), *A Restless Mind: Essays in Honor of Amos Perlmutter* (London: Frank Cass, 1998), pp. 80–103.

26. Dore Gold, 'Middle East Missile Proliferation, Israeli Missile Defense, and the ABM Treaty Debate', *Jerusalem Letter*, 430 (May 2000), pp. 6–7; Gerald Steinberg, 'Re-examining Israel's Security Doctrine', *RUSI International Security Review 1999* (London: Royal United Services Institute for Defense Analysis, 1999), pp. 215–44.

27. B. Lasenesky, 'Friendly Restraint: US–Israel Relations During the Gulf Crisis of 1990–1991', *Middle East Review of International Affairs* (MERIA), 3, 2 (June 1999).

28. Inbar, 'The Shift from Self-Reliance', p. 80.

29. Both citations in ibid., pp. 87–8.

30. Thus, in the wake of the Madrid Conference, Israel participated in the Arms Control and Regional Security (ACRS) discussions and in response to American pressure in October 1991 for the first time accepted the Missile Technology Control Regime (MTCR); in September 1992 Israel agreed to sign the Chemical Weapons Convention (CWC), thereby relinquishing its previous insistence on prior Arab signature, and by the end of 1993 had begun to comply with international demands that it report its arms sales to the United Nations' arms registrar. Even its nuclear policies seemed to be moving (albeit much more cautiously) in the same direction, indicating a willingness to revise its previous adamantly negative attitude towards the Non-Proliferation Treaty.

31. See, for example, Rabin's Knesset speech of January 1993, cited in David Makovsky,

Making Peace with the PLO: The Rabin Government's Road to the Oslo Accord (Boulder, CO: Westview Press, 1996), p. 113.

32. See, for example, Ze'ev Schiff, Peace with Security: Israel's Minimal Security Requirements in Negotiations with Syria, Policy Paper no. 34 (Washington, DC: Washington Institute for Near East Policy, 1993), p. 101.

33. Schiff, 'Israel After the War', p. 27.

34. Especially noteworthy, in this context, is Ariel Levite's Offense and Defense in Israeli Strategy (Hebrew; Tel Aviv: Jaffee Center for Strategic Studies, 1988, and also in English; Boulder, CO: Westview Press, 1989), which argued – inter alia – that, in a battlefield likely to be saturated with precision-guided munitions (PGMs), the IDF would have no alternative but to revolutionize its entire mode of operations and hence to prefer defense to offense. See also Eliot Cohen, Michael Eisenstadt and Andrew Bacevich, Knives, Tanks and Missiles: Israel's Security Revolution (Washington, DC: Washington Institute for Near East Policy, 1998), pp. 78–9, 84–6, 126–7.

35. See Reuven Pedahtzur, The Arrow System and the Active Defense Against Ballistic Missiles, Memorandum No. 42 (Hebrew; Tel Aviv: Jaffee Center for Strategic Studies, October 1993).

36. Martin Navias, Saddam's Scud War and Ballistic Missile Proliferation (London: Centre for Defence Studies, 1991); Anthony Cordesman and Abraham Wagner, The Lessons of Modern War, Vol. IV: The Gulf War (Boulder, CO: Westview Press, 1994), p. 869.

37. Israel State Comptroller, Annual Report, No. 44 (Hebrew; Jerusalem: Government Printing House, 1995), pp. 938–75.

38. Thus, David Ivri stated that one of his own conclusions from the Gulf War was that 'intelligence must receive priority'. Interview in Ba-Machaneh (Hebrew weekly), 6 January 1993. See also interview with Barak in Jerusalem Post, 5 September 1994, p. 7.

39. See Ilan Berman, Partnership in Transition: US–Israel Strategic Cooperation Beyond the Cold War (Washington, DC: Jewish Institute for National Security Affairs, 2000), p. 33.

40. Arrow-1 was successfully tested late in 1994, as was Arrow-2 in August 1997 and in November 1999. By March 2000, the entire system (which by then had cost $1.3 billion – most of which had been provided by the USA) was declared operational.

41. Avi Kober, 'Israel's Doctrine of Military Decision: A Paradigm in Crisis?', in Efraim Karsh (ed.), Between War and Peace: Dilemmas of Israeli Security (London: Frank Cass, 1996), p. 207. See also Ze'ev Bonen, 'Sophisticated Conventional War', in Advanced Technology and Future War, BESA Security and Policy Studies, No. 28 (Ramat Gan: BESA Center for Strategic Studies, 1996), pp. 19–30.

42. Hatzofeh (Hebrew daily), 3 December 1996. Since 1995 the age 'ceiling' for reserve duty has been steadily lowered from 54 to 45.

43. Stuart A. Cohen, 'The IDF: From a "People's Army" to a "Professional Military"' Armed Forces & Society, 21, 2 (Winter 1995), pp. 237–54. Also see report in Ha'aretz, 25 July 2000, p. A5.

44. Maarachot devoted its entire issue No. 358 (published in April 1998) to an analysis and description of Aviv Neurim, including an introduction by then Vice-COS Shaul Mofaz and articles by other senior officers.

45. Ze'ev Schiff, 'A Quiet Re-Organization in the General Staff', Ha'aretz, 9 July 1998, p. B1.

46. This theme permeates analyses of the tactical and operational lessons of the Gulf conflict soon thereafter published in Maarachot, e.g. 'Objectives, Fire-support and "Smart Weapons"', 28 (February 1993), pp. 2–8; Col. Dr Yitzhak Ben Yisrael, 'Back to the Future', 329 (April 1993), pp. 2–5; and Dr Ze'ev Bonen, 'Towards Three-Tier Warfare', 340 (April 1995), pp. 2–10.

47. Interview with Maj.-Gen. Shalom Haggai (Head of Quartermaster Branch),

Ha'aretz, 13 May 1993, p. B2.

48. If anything, it was the Yugoslavia campaign that really counted. See Yitzhak Ben Yisrael, 'Technology and Decision – Thoughts on the IDF in the Wake of Kosovo', *Maarachot*, 371 (July 2000), pp. 34–43.

49. Zvi Ofer and Avi Kober (eds), *Quality and Quantity in Military Buildup* (Hebrew; Tel Aviv: Ministry of Defense Publications, 1985); Cohen *et al.*, *Knives, Tanks and Missiles*, pp. 57–62.

50. Dan Meridor, 'The Political–Strategic Challenge to Israel' (Hebrew; paper delivered at Tel Aviv University, 7 May 1991), *Dapei Elazar*, 14 (Tel Aviv, 1992), pp. 111–27.

51. Stuart A. Cohen, 'The Peace Process and its Impact on the Development of a "Smaller and Smarter" IDF', *Israel Affairs*, 1 (1995), pp. 1–21; for a recent assessment see Anthony H. Cordesman, *Peace and War: The Arab-Israeli Military Balance Enters the 21st Century* (Westport, CT: Paeger, 2002), pp. 199–201.

52. See Ya'akov Lifshitz, *The Economics of Security: General Theory and the Israeli Case* (Hebrew; Jerusalem: Jerusalem Institute for the Study of Israel, 2000), p. 261.

53. See interview with Maj.-Gen. Matan Vilnai in *Davar* (Hebrew daily), 20 April 1995 and with Maj.-Gen. Doron Almog in *Ha'aretz*, 22 September 1999, p. B4. Hence, although Egypt still figures in IDF contingency planning, the General Staff has seriously considered disbanding its Southern Command altogether.

54. E.g., interviews with current Vice-Chief of Staff, Gen. Uzi Dayan, *Ha'aretz*, 3 February 1999, p. A5, and with Gen. Shlomo Yannai (CO, IDF Planning Branch), *Shiryon*, 6 (October 1999), pp. 8–9.

55. Official IDF transcript. See also report of Shahak's lecture at Tel Aviv University in *Ha'aretz*, 15 July 1997, p. A3.

56. Charles S. Liebman and Eliezer Don-Yehiyah, *Civil Religion in Israel: Traditional Religion and Political Culture in the Jewish State* (Berkeley, CA: University of California Press, 1983).

57. Uri Ben-Eliezer, *The Making of Israeli Militarism* (Bloomington, IN: Indiana University Press, 1998).

58. Moshe Lissak and Dan Horowitz, *Trouble in Utopia: The Overburdened Polity of Israel* (Albany, NY: SUNY Press, 1989), pp. 236–9.

59. Reuven Gal and Stuart A. Cohen, 'Israel: Still Waiting in the Wings', in Charles Moskos, John Allen Williams and David R. Segal (eds), *The Postmodern Military: Armed Forces after the Cold War* (New York: Oxford University Press, 2000), pp. 224–51.

60. For the text, see Asa Kasher, *Military Ethics* (Hebrew; Tel Aviv: Ministry of Defense, 1996), pp. 232–7.

61. Estimates of the numbers of people who actually left Israeli conurbations during the war vary widely. While some studies suggest 13% (Asher Arian, 'Security and Political Attitudes: The Gulf War', in Alpher, *War in the Gulf*, p. 303), others put the figure as high as 34% (Solomon, *Coping with War-Induced Stress*, p. 46). However, even the latter figure is probably lower than, say, the proportion of evacuees from Tehran during the 'war of the cities'. Ben-Meir, 'Israeli Home Front in the Gulf War', p. 339.

62. See, for example, interview with Barak in *Davar*, 5 April 1993, p. 21 and Rabin in *Davar*, 26 May 1994, p. 16.

63. Over 40% of the residents of Kiryat Shemoneh, the largest single conurbation in the eastern Galilee, are estimated to have fled the city during the PLO Katyusha attacks of the summer of 1981. Ze'ev Schiff and Ehud Ya'ari, *Israel's Lebanon War* (New York: Simon & Schuster, 1984), p. 36.

64. Dan Horowitz, 'Strategic Limitations of "A Nation in Arms"', *Armed Forces & Society*, 13, 2 (Winter 1987), pp. 277–94.

65. For an insider's view of Israeli perceptions of these incidents: Danny Naveh, *Government Secrets* (Hebrew; Tel Aviv: Yediot Aharonof, 1999), pp. 162–8. The author was Secretary to the Cabinet between 1996 and 1999.

66. Of these, undoubtedly the most significant has been the realization that, in a future war, the panic likely to be induced by missile attacks on Israel's rear – together with the massive traffic jams to which they are bound to give rise – might impede IDF reserve mobilization schedules. See Mofaz's statement to this effect, reported in *Ha'aretz*, 13 January 1999, p. A4; and Ron Ben Yishai, 'Israel No Longer Relies Solely on Reservists', *Yediot Aharonot* (Hebrew daily), 13 January 1999, p. 11.

67. Dan Meron, 'If There is an IDF – Let it Appear Immediately', *Ha'aretz*, 14 February 1991, p. B2.

68. Ben-Meir, 'Israeli Home Front in the Gulf War', p. 335. For Shai's own evaluation of his role, see his 'The Communications War – Ten Lessons', *Maarachot* (Hebrew), 374–5 (February 2001), pp. 74–7.

69. Gad Barzilai and Efraim Inbar, 'Do Wars have an Impact? Israeli Public Opinion after the Gulf War', *Jerusalem Journal of International Relations*, 14 (March 1992), pp. 44–64. Comparing the results of polls conducted immediately before the invasion of Kuwait and soon after the end of the fighting, Barzilai and Inbar conclude: 'The surprising finding is that what must be considered a traumatic event – the Gulf War – had little impact on Israeli public opinion … The Gulf War has neither strengthened the dovish trend present until 1990, nor has it reinforced hawkishness' (p. 62).

70. Asher Arian, Michal Shamir and Raphael Ventura, 'Public Opinion and Political Change: Israel and the Intifadah', *Comparative Politics*, 24 (1992), pp. 317–35.

71. Asher Arian, 'Security and Political Attitudes: The Gulf War', in Alpher, *War in the Gulf*, p. 325. See also the same author's *Security Threatened: Surveying Israeli Opinion on Peace and War* (Cambridge: Cambridge University Press, 1995), pp. 81–8.

72. Arian, *Security Threatened*, pp. 57–62, 91–127.

73. Thomas Risse-Kapen, 'Public Opinion, Domestic Structure, and Foreign Policy in Liberal Democracies', *World Politics*, 43 (July 1991), pp. 479–512.

Part IV:

The United States

6

A Squandered Opportunity?
The Decision to End the Gulf War

THOMAS G. MAHNKEN

INTRODUCTION

In his autobiography, Colin Powell quotes approvingly Fred Iklé's classic book on war termination, *Every War Must End*. He recalls being particularly taken with Iklé's observation that in war fighting often goes on beyond the point at which it should rationally end. Indeed, Powell had key passages of the book copied and circulated to Secretary of Defense Dick Cheney, National Security Advisor Brent Scowcroft, and the Joint Chiefs of Staff.[1]

Powell's professed recognition of the fact that one should not start a war without first deciding how to finish it is ironic, given the confusion and lack of deliberation that surrounded the decision to halt the Gulf War. For all the effort President Bush and his advisors took in planning the liberation of Kuwait, they spent remarkably little time thinking about how to ensure a durable postwar settlement. Powell's fear of exceeding the culminating point of victory is also ironic, since, if anything, coalition forces stopped short of achieving a decisive victory, based at least in part upon his advice.

Determining when to end a war is one of the greatest challenges that soldiers and statesmen face. This chapter argues that the United States chose to end the Gulf War prematurely, robbing the coalition of the opportunity to translate a lopsided battlefield victory into a durable postwar settlement. While coalition forces succeeded in expelling the Iraqi army from Kuwait, they failed in the overarching goal of compelling Saddam Hussein to do their will. Because of this, Saddam remained in power, a continuing threat to the stability and security of the region.

Defenders of the decision to halt the war after 100 hours of ground combat frequently posit a false choice between this and a march to Baghdad to overthrow Saddam Hussein. In fact, the United States possessed a range of options to pressure Saddam into leaving office, or at least admitting defeat. The real choice was between ending the war before coalition forces had completed their mission and pursuing options to compel Iraq to accept defeat. The time to do so was prior to the declaration of a ceasefire. Once the US government announced a halt to military operations, its leverage over Saddam evaporated.

WAR AND WAR TERMINATION

Soldiers and statesmen must never lose sight of the fact that wars are fought to achieve political aims. These may include not only narrow objectives such as the destruction of an enemy army and occupation of territory, but broader considerations such as the achievement of a more favorable postwar situation. As Basil Liddell-Hart reminds us, 'The object of war is a better state of peace – even if only from your own point of view. Hence it is essential to conduct war with constant regard to the peace you desire.'[2]

In his masterpiece, *On War*, Carl von Clausewitz defined war as 'an act of force to compel our enemy to do our will'.[3] This formulation speaks not only to the enduring nature of war, but also to the preconditions for concluding a conflict successfully. Whatever the specific objectives of a particular war, the overall aim is always to compel the adversary to do our will. For Clausewitz, this usually involved destroying his forces, occupying his territory, and – most importantly – breaking his will to resist.[4]

In a war fought for limited aims, the decision to end a war must be a mutual one, the result of bargaining between the victor and the vanquished.[5] Indeed, because the losing side frequently has the ability to prolong the struggle, it is often the one that holds the key to ending a conflict. Compelling an adversary to concede is therefore of paramount importance. As Fred Iklé has written:

> for any war effort – offensive or defensive – that is supposed to serve long-term national objectives, the most essential question is how the enemy might be forced to surrender, or failing that, what sort of bargain must be struck with him to terminate the war.[6]

Battlefield victories are an insufficient ingredient of a lasting peace.[7] They do not themselves determine the outcome of wars; rather, they provide opportunities for the victor to translate battlefield results into political outcomes. Two things in particular must occur for military force to be decisive: the defeated power must accept defeat and the victor must formulate a settlement that accommodates the interests of all concerned, including the loser. In concrete terms, this means that either the incumbent government must accept responsibility for defeat while retaining its legitimacy, or it must be replaced with a cooperative yet credible successor.[8] If the losing side does not accept the war's outcome, then it may harbor designs to alter the *status quo* some time in the future. As Clausewitz put it, 'the defeated state often considers the outcome [of the war] merely a transitory evil, for which a remedy may still be found in political considerations at some later date'.[9]

Why a nation concedes in war is one of the most important yet least understood questions in strategic theory. Clausewitz argued that the decision is based at least in part upon a 'rational calculus'. As he wrote:

> Since war is not an act of senseless passion but is controlled by its political object, the value of this object must determine the sacrifices to be made for it in *magnitude* and also in *duration*. Once the expenditure of effort exceeds the value of the political object, the object must be renounced and peace must follow.[10]

A purely rational approach to war termination is clearly unrealistic. States are not unitary actors and possess limited knowledge of their own capabilities and those of the enemy.[11]

Moreover, what we know about why states surrender seems to indicate that it is based not upon the damage that their forces have already sustained, but rather upon the leadership's expectations of future punishment. While the definitive study of the decision to surrender has yet to be written, Robert McQuie's analysis of battle outcomes at the tactical level of war is suggestive. His study of 52 battles fought between 1941 and 1982 shows that the principal condition associated with the decision to surrender was not the casualties that the losing side had suffered, but rather the victor's use of maneuver to put him in a favorable position to launch a future attack. In other words, because commanders are forward-looking, the recognition of defeat appears to arise from a look to the future, not the past.[12]

These findings corroborate Patton's famous aphorism that battles are lost in the mind of the commander before they are lost on the battlefield.[13] In other words, the ultimate object of war is to create an effect – a sense of hopelessness – in the mind of the adversary. The successful strategist forces his foe to believe that if he does not concede, then things will get much worse – for him, his regime and the state. It seems probable, for example, that Slobodan Milosevic agreed to withdraw from Kosovo not because of the limited damage NATO had inflicted upon Serbia, but because he calculated that his situation would deteriorate further if the conflict continued.[14]

There is also a clear relationship between how far one goes militarily and what one demands politically. The greater the demands one makes upon the loser, the less incentive he has to concede and the greater the effort that will be required to force him to surrender.[15] During the Gulf War, the United States did not go far enough militarily to get Saddam Hussein to concede defeat. To secure Saddam's cooperation, it needed either to press on militarily or to back off politically.

TERMINATING THE GULF WAR

The broad outlines of the Gulf War are well known. On 2 August 1990, Iraq invaded Kuwait in a bid to seize the emirate's wealth and secure regional hegemony. American diplomatic skill, combined with Baghdad's audacity, led to the formation of a broad coalition aimed at expelling Iraq from the emirate. This included not only traditional US friends and allies and key regional states, but also regimes that were traditionally neutral or even hostile toward the United States. On 15 January 1991, President George Bush signed National Security Directive 54, authorizing the use of military force to achieve four political objectives:

> [T]o effect the immediate, complete, and unconditional with-drawal of all Iraqi forces from Kuwait; to restore Kuwait's legiti-mate government; to protect the lives of American citizens abroad; and to promote the security and the stability of the Persian Gulf.

Bush specified that 'military operations will come to an end only when I have determined that [these] objectives ... have been met'.[16]

Determining when the first three objectives had been achieved was a relatively straightforward matter. By contrast, judging how to promote the security and stability of the region required keen political judgement. Stopping short of achieving this objective would leave Iraq a threat to its neighbors; going too far could potentially weaken Iraq to such a point that it might collapse. Left unstated was the goal of removing Saddam Hussein from power. While the US government never made Saddam's overthrow an explicit objective, it is clear that Bush and his advisors believed that it was Saddam who was the cause of instability in the Gulf and were at best ambivalent about leav-ing him in power.

On 16 January, coalition forces launched a massive air cam-paign against the Iraqi army in Kuwait as well as targets in Iraq. Over the next 38 days, attacks from the air inflicted considerable damage on Iraqi conventional forces and logistics in Kuwait as well as military infrastructure within Iraq itself. Early on the morning of 24 February, coalition forces began a ground campaign to liberate Kuwait. The US Central Command (USCENTCOM) plan envisioned marine and Arab forces fixing the Iraqi army south of Kuwait City while the US army's VII and XVIII Corps, together with British and French forces, enveloped them. Acting in concert, coalition ground forces would trap and destroy Iraq's three heavy Republican Guard divisions before they could escape across the Euphrates. In the event, marine forces succeeded beyond all expectations, while the VII Corps' attack took longer than anticipated to develop. The marines advanced so rapidly upon Kuwait City that Republican Guard units were unable to move south to reinforce the Iraqi front lines. Instead of fixing Iraqi forces, the marines became a piston that drove them out of the Kuwait theater ahead of the advancing VII and XVIII Corps.

The ground campaign began achieving results almost immediately. Iraqi forces, led by III Corps, began to withdraw from Kuwait at 10.30 p.m. local time (2.30 p.m. Washington time) on 25 February. Iraqi radio announced the move early the following morning.[17] In Baghdad, Iraqi Foreign Minister Tariq Aziz contacted the Soviet ambassador with a message calling upon Mikhail Gorbachev to broker a ceasefire with the United Nations. As Bush saw it, 'Saddam had declared victory and was trying to save as much of his army as he could.'[18]

Deciding When to Say When

At 8 p.m. that evening, Bush met with his top national security advisors to review the progress of the war. Powell predicted that coalition forces would envelop the withdrawing Iraqi force within two days. Scowcroft saw the encirclement and destruction of Iraqi forces as less important than ensuring that Saddam Hussein personally agreed to abide by all the United Nations resolutions against Iraq. His urgings led the US government to announce that the only way for Saddam to convince Washington of his seriousness would be for him to 'personally and publicly' agree to US demands and fulfill the conditions of all UN resolutions.[19]

Bush, for one, seemed intent on continuing the war until coalition forces had achieved a decisive victory over Iraq. That night he wrote in his diary:

It seems to me that we may get to a place where we have to choose between solidarity at the UN and ending this thing definitively. I am for the latter because our credibility is at stake ... We're not going to allow a sloppy ending where this guy emerges saving face.[20]

Despite Bush's desire for a decisive outcome, pressure to end the war was even then building. On the evening of 25 February, coalition air forces pummeled a column of fleeing Iraqi troops on Mutlah Ridge. The incident, widely reported in the press as the 'highway of death', created the impression that the war had become a rout.[21] Leaders in Washington began to fear that press coverage of the war could sap support at home and split the coalition.

As the ground campaign continued, Bush grasped for a way to end the war on terms favoring the United States. In his diary on 26 February he wrote:

We've got to find a clean end, and I keep saying, how do we end this thing? ... You can't use the word surrender – the Arabs don't like that apparently. How do we quit? How do we get them to lay down their arms? How do we safeguard civilians? And how do we get on with our role with credibility, hoping to bring security to the Gulf?[22]

As the war progressed, an ever-widening gap emerged between what was occurring in Kuwait and Iraq and what decision-makers in Washington *thought* was happening. Despite the fact that the US government had at its disposal the world's most sophisticated intelligence systems and communications networks, Bush and his advisors lacked a clear view of what was taking place in the theater. They believed that the ground campaign was unfolding according to plan, only more rapidly than anticipated. They also predicted that coalition forces would bar the door leading out of the theater at Basra within a day or two. What they did not understand was that the marines' rapid advance, coupled with the slow progress of the VII Corps, meant that much of the Iraqi force would potentially be able to escape encirclement and destruction.[23] The phenomenon that

Clausewitz dubbed 'friction' would eventually play an important role in the decision to halt the war.

As statesmen in Washington began to contemplate ending the war, soldiers in Saudi Arabia and Kuwait grappled with ways to encircle the fleeing Iraqis. The advance of coalition ground forces began driving the Iraqis into a pocket across the Euphrates River from Basra. Iraqi units put up a stiff defense while also attempting to withdraw over more than 20 bridges and causeways over the Shatt al Arab and Euphrates River. Interdicting them by air had proven impossible; the only way to seal off the theater would be to block all exits with ground forces. Accordingly, the commander of the US army's VII Corps, Lieutenant-General Fred Franks, positioned his forces to launch a double envelopment of the remaining Iraqi forces on the morning of 28 February. With the first Cavalry Division to the north and the first Infantry Division to the south, the first and third Armored and British first Armored Divisions would envelop the remaining Iraqi forces in the theater. Franks estimated that the battle would be over by that evening.[24] In the XVIII Corps' sector, Major-General Binford Peay planned to airlift an entire brigade of his 101st Air Assault Division across the Euphrates and set it down north of Basra, severing the Republican Guard's last escape route. Major-General Barry McCaffrey's 24th Infantry Division would swing east to seal off the Euphrates valley.[25]

Friction Triumphant

On the evening of 27 February, coordination both within the theater and between the theater and Washington broke down. In retrospect, it is clear that the Commander-in-Chief of USCENTCOM, General H. Norman Schwarzkopf, did not know where his forces were located. Similarly, Powell did not inform the President and his advisors that coalition ground forces had yet to encircle the remaining Iraqi forces in Kuwait. As a result, decision-makers in Washington lacked a clear understanding of the situation on the ground. When Bush decided to end the war, he did so under the misapprehension that US forces had already achieved their objectives.

At 9 p.m. in Riyadh, Schwarzkopf gave a press conference, soon dubbed the 'mother of all briefings'. Using triumphal language, he claimed that 29 Iraqi divisions had been rendered completely ineffective. He also announced: 'The gate [leading out of Kuwait] is closed. There is no way out of here.' Announcing that US forces had accomplished their mission, he added: 'when the decision-makers come to the decision that there should be a ceasefire, nobody will be happier than me'. He also announced that the allies had no intention of marching to Baghdad.[26]

Schwarzkopf's briefing gave decision-makers in Washington the false impression that coalition forces had achieved their goal of encircling the Republican Guard when they had not. The briefing, which occurred with little coordination with Washington, did a great deal to limit the administration's political options. By indicating that the coalition was ready – even eager – to end the war, Schwarzkopf's statements took pressure off Saddam. Moreover, by portraying the war as a one-sided rout, the General gave ammunition to those who wanted to halt the war. Schwarzkopf in effect declared victory a day early, robbing his civilian superiors of the opportunity to coerce Saddam.[27]

Shortly after Schwarzkopf gave his briefing, Bush met with his advisors to discuss ending the war. The meeting that followed lacked a thorough discussion of the situation on the ground and the extent to which the USA could translate it into a more stable situation in the Gulf. There was general agreement that the United States had met its objectives. Coalition forces had driven the Iraqi army out of Kuwait. In addition, the air and ground campaigns had eroded significantly Iraq's offensive capability. Given the circumstances, it would have made perfect sense for the United States to continue military operations until Iraq conceded. The United States needed to exert unrelenting pressure upon Saddam to translate its operational advantage into strategic success.[28] Instead, Bush's advisors argued that it was time to call a halt to the war. Powell was concerned that the United States could lose the moral high ground by continuing past the 'rational' stopping point. Scowcroft and Cheney also wanted to avoid the perception that the United States was a bully beating up a helpless Iraq.

In considering whether to end the war, Bush and his advisors were operating under the misperception (fostered by Schwarzkopf's news conference) that the Republican Guard had already been encircled and all but destroyed. Nor was Schwarzkopf alone in failing to paint an accurate picture of the situation in Kuwait and southern Iraq. The CENTCOM daily intelligence summary for 27 February reported that 'the Republican Guards are encircled ... They have few options other than surrender or destruction.' The Joint Chiefs of Staff reiterated this message in a briefing to Cheney the same day.[29]

Given the rosy picture of the situation on the ground, Bush asked his advisors whether it was time to stop the war. As he later wrote:

> It looked as if we would trap or destroy the remains of Saddam's army in Kuwait, but he did not seem willing to capitulate. Eventually, I decided that it was our choice, not Saddam's; we would declare an end once I was sure we had met all our military objectives and fulfilled the UN resolutions.[30]

The tendency to stop short of victory based upon faulty information is hardly unique to this war. As Clausewitz noted:

> There is still another factor that can bring military action to a standstill: imperfect knowledge of the situation. The only situation a commander can fully know is his own; his opponent's he can only know from unreliable intelligence. His evaluation, therefore, may be mistaken and can lead him to suppose that the initiative lies with the enemy when in fact it remains with him.[31]

Powell suggested consulting Schwarzkopf, calling him from a secure phone in the Oval Office. Rather than asking him whether he felt it was time to end the war, Powell instead told him that things were getting difficult in Washington and that Bush was thinking of going on the air to announce a ceasefire effective from 5 a.m. on 28 February and asked whether he had any objections. Schwarzkopf, who yielded to Powell repeatedly throughout the war, said he could accept the ceasefire, but wanted to consult with his subordinates.[32]

In an interview after the war, Schwarzkopf claimed that his

'recommendation had been ... to continue the march. I mean, we had them in a rout and could have continued to wreak great destruction on them. We could have completely closed the doors and made it in fact a battle of annihilation.'[33] There is no evidence, however, that Schwarzkopf objected when Powell informed him that a ceasefire was being considered.

Just as Powell informed rather than consulted Schwarzkopf, Schwarzkopf presented the decision to end the war as a *fait accompli*. The navy, air force and marine corps leaders did not object; Lieutenant-General John Yeosock, the Ground Component Commander, realized that US army forces had yet to encircle the Republican Guard but did not speak up.[34] Schwarzkopf instructed Yeosock to separate allied forces from the Iraqis and assume a defensive posture.

The closer one got to the front lines, the more questionable the decision to halt the war seemed. Yeosock did not ask Franks or any of his division commanders whether their forces had achieved their objectives. If he had, he would have learnt that they had not.[35] Both Peay and McCaffrey were stunned by the decision because they had yet to destroy the Republican Guard.[36]

When Bush reconvened his advisors at 6 p.m., Powell reported that Schwarzkopf favored ending the war the following day, making it a five-day war. Nobody in the room disagreed. Cheney believed that US forces had basically achieved their objectives. Secretary of State James Baker concurred, but felt that too little attention had been paid to the future of Saddam's regime.[37] Scowcroft subsequently said he had misgivings, but did not voice them.[38] Bush therefore decided to announce the 'suspension of offensive combat operations' effective midnight Washington time, or 8 a.m., 28 February on the battlefield, making it a 100-hour ground war. The term was an explicit concession of the fact that Iraq had yet to surrender.

It is clear that, to the extent that Bush and his advisors were responding to pressure, it was self-generated. At the time they decided to halt the war, public and congressional support for US military action remained strong. Nor were US allies pressing for a halt. Indeed, it was only after the decision was made that US coalition partners were notified.

Outside Bush's immediate circle, there were those who questioned whether US forces had indeed accomplished their objectives, but they were not consulted. Analysts at the Central Intelligence Agency felt that another day was needed to encircle the Iraqi army. More significantly, Under-Secretary of Defense for Policy Paul Wolfowitz opposed a ceasefire because he believed it would reduce dramatically the pressure the coalition was exerting over Saddam. He instead favored halting without announcing an end to hostilities.[39]

The decision to end the war based upon the presumed envelopment of Iraqi forces in Kuwait is evidence of the fact that the US leadership failed to understand Iraq's true center of gravity; the US political and military leadership acted as if it were the Republican Guard in Kuwait, while in fact it was Saddam and his regime. Inflicting damage upon Iraqi forces was a means to influence Saddam's strategic calculus. To many in the American political and military leadership, however, it became an end in itself. In fact, ejecting the Iraqi army from Kuwait was but one of four objectives. More important was the need to improve the stability of the region. While attrition of the Iraqi army could contribute to this goal, weakening the Iraqi military would not by itself lead to stability and security. If this were indeed a goal, then Saddam would have to be removed, or at least cowed.

The surest way to coerce Saddam would have been to continue to pressure him. Clausewitz described the importance of exerting psychological pressure upon a foe in the following passage:

> The situation is completely different when a defeated army is being pursued. Resistance becomes difficult, indeed sometimes impossible, as a consequence of battle casualties, loss of order and courage, and anxiety about the retreat. The pursuer who in the former case had to move with circumspection, almost groping like a blind man, can now advance with the arrogance of the fortunate and the confidence of a demigod. The faster his pace, the greater the speed with which events will run along their predetermined course: this is the primary area where psychological forces will increase and multiply without being rigidly bound to the weights and measures of the material world.[40]

Bush had regrets about the decision to end the war. As he wrote in his diary on 28 February:

> After my speech last night, Baghdad radio started broadcasting that we've been forced to capitulate. I see on television that public opinion in Jordan and in the streets of Baghdad is that they have won. It is such a canard, so little, but it's what concerns me. It hasn't been a clean end – there is no battleship Missouri surrender. This is what's missing to make this akin to WWII, to separate Kuwait from Korea and Vietnam.[41]

Bush was at best ambivalent about the limited nature of US political objectives in the war. He clearly hoped that Iraq's humiliating defeat would trigger a popular revolt or military coup that would topple Saddam. As Baker put it, 'Strategically, the real objective was to eject Iraq from Kuwait in a manner that would destroy Saddam's offensive military capabilities and make his fall from power likely.'[42] Several Arab governments predicted – incorrectly – that Saddam Hussein would not be able to survive such a dramatic defeat. Bush and his advisors were heartened when the US intelligence community identified two of Saddam's personal aircraft at an airport in Baghdad, raising the possibility that he might be preparing to flee the country.[43] While Bush wanted Saddam out of power, he was unwilling to take the steps necessary to weaken or remove him. Rather than continuing to pressure Saddam until he was on one of those planes on his way out of Iraq, he decided to leave the strategic outcome of the war to chance.

The decision to change the timing of the ceasefire to achieve a nice, round number had considerable repercussions in the theater. At 2 a.m., Powell informed Schwarzkopf that the ceasefire had been finalized, but that it had been moved back to 8 a.m. local time. Powell also expressed the administration's desire that the Iraqis be forced to abandon their vehicles and walk back to Iraq.[44] Schwarzkopf voiced no objection. The gap between the general's understanding of the disposition of his forces and their actual location became clear when he informed his deputy, Lieutenant-General Cal Waller, of the decision to cease hostilities. Waller was stunned by the news and informed Schwarzkopf that a substantial number of Iraqis were continuing to escape Kuwait.[45]

Schwarzkopf was forced to call Powell back to tell him that coalition forces had not encircled the Iraqis and that a ceasefire would allow Iraqi armored vehicles, including Republican Guard T-72s, to continue to escape.[46] Powell, in turn, informed the President and his advisors that the gate was still open. Their response was nonchalant. As he later wrote:

> Although we were all taken slightly aback, no one felt that what we had heard changed the basic equation. The back of the Iraqi army had been broken. What was left of it was retreating north. There was no need to fight a battle of annihilation to see how many more combatants on both sides could be killed.[47]

Powell's statement speaks volumes of the US leadership's casual attitude toward war termination and its misunderstanding of the strategic center of gravity. Bush and his advisors decided to end the war based at least in part upon the misapprehension that CENTCOM had enveloped the Republican Guard. Yet when they learnt that US forces had not accomplished their mission, they did not revisit their earlier decision. Nor was there an effort to link the end-state of the war to the need to exert continuing pressure on Saddam. It mattered that US forces had expelled Iraq from Kuwait and inflicted damage on the Iraqi army, but it also mattered how the United States positioned its forces at the end of the war.

After the war it became clear that half of the Republican Guard's equipment had escaped destruction and that the vast majority of Iraqi troops had been south of Basra in the path of the army's planned advance.[48] Up to 100,000 Iraqi soldiers, including up to 70 per cent of the Hammurabi Republican Guard division, escaped to Basra and then fled along Shatt al Arab to Al Qurna, while others escaped on the causeway across the Hawr al Hammar. The US government later estimated that 842 tanks, including 365 T-72s, and 1,412 armored vehicles had been able to flee the theater.[49]

The View from Baghdad

The bureaucratic confusion in Washington that led to a unilateral ceasefire is only part of the story. To analyze the effectiveness of US war termination strategy – to assess how well the United States compelled Saddam to do its will – we need to look at the situation in Baghdad.

Reconstructing Saddam's state of mind is extremely difficult. There are exceedingly few credible sources of information on his mental state during the war. Yet such insight is vital if we are to evaluate the success of the US war termination strategy. The most compelling evidence comes from General Wafiq al-Samarrai, who served as director of Iraqi military intelligence during the Gulf War. According to him, Saddam worried that the coalition might march on Baghdad and hunt him down, as US forces had Manuel Noriega in Panama. Bush's rhetoric comparing Saddam to Hitler doubtless fueled this fear. Al-Samarrai paints a picture of the Iraqi leader as increasingly anxious, depressed and desperate as the war wore on.[50] As he put it, Saddam was near a state of complete mental and physical collapse and believed that his downfall was imminent:

> Before the cease-fire was announced his morale was very deteriorated and he was very tense and tired. He was almost completely collapsed ... He was in very poor condition and at that moment he was really saved by Bush's offer of cease-fire. Before the cease-fire, he felt his doom was very close by. As I just said, he sat before me and he was almost in tears, not crying, but almost in tears ... He said, 'We do not know what God will bring upon us tomorrow.' This shows that he was virtually collapsing. So, he was at the lowest.[51]

It seems likely that continued US pressure on his regime could at this point have convinced him to leave office. Instead, Washington's decision to halt the war provided an instant tonic. As al-Samarrai recalls:

> Within two hours [of him learning of the ceasefire], Saddam came in with his escort and media people to our headquarters and started to issue orders by phone. He became a hero and he

felt that everything was now subdued and there is no more danger, and well, we have this legend in our history. He was feeling himself as a great, great hero. He started to go like, 'We won, we won!' His morale was boosted from rank zero to one hundred! ... He was laughing and kidding and joking and talking about Bush.[52]

By declaring a unilateral end to the war, the United States sharply reduced its leverage over Saddam. Soon after the ceasefire, Saddam went on the air claiming:

> O Iraqis, you triumphed when you stood with all this vigor against the armies of thirty countries ... You have succeeded in demolishing the aura of the United States, the empire of evil, terror, and aggression ... The Guards have broken the backbone of their aggressors and thrown them beyond their borders. We are confident that President Bush would never have accepted a cease-fire had he not been informed by his military leaders of the need to preserve the forces fleeing the fist of the heroic men of the Republican Guard.[53]

Like Nasser in 1956 and Sadat in 1973, Saddam was able to turn defeat into victory. Al-Samarrai argues that 'Saddam, even today, looks at himself as victorious.'[54]

Reaching a Settlement

The confusion that marked the decision to end the Gulf War continued as the United States attempted to craft a postwar settlement. In the period following the decision to announce a ceasefire, the United States did little to translate its tremendous battlefield advantage into leverage at the bargaining table. Rather, it squandered its influence and in the process reduced its chances of achieving a lasting peace. Nobody in a position of authority in Washington or Riyadh had given much thought to how to end the war; almost everything had to be improvised. On the night of 28 February, Schwarzkopf called General Khaled bin Sultan, the Joint Forces Commander, to tell him that Bush wanted the two of them to meet with the Iraqis as soon as possible.[55]

Khaled assumed that they would be arranging a formal surrender, like that of the Japanese in Tokyo Bay in 1945. However, it was not until 11 p.m. on the night of 1 March that Schwarzkopf and Khaled met to discuss the meeting. Even then, Khaled's memoirs make it clear that little thought had gone into planning the negotiations. As he put it, 'arrangements for the Safwan meeting were made in a hurry with apparently little regard for the longer-term consequences'.[56] The venue had yet to be determined. Schwarzkopf originally proposed meeting aboard an American aircraft carrier, an idea Khaled vetoed. It was only then that Schwarzkopf proposed holding the talks at Safwan, which he incorrectly believed to be under American occupation. Similarly, it was not until the night before the meeting that the United States learnt that Iraq would be represented by Lieutenant-General Sultan Hashim Ahmad al-Jabburi, the army's Deputy Chief of Staff for Operations, and Lieutenant-General Salah Abbud Mahmud al-Daghastani, the commander of the Iraqi III Corps.[57]

The haphazard approach continued at Safwan. The meeting was termed a 'military-to-military' exchange, not a formal surrender, in recognition of the fact that Iraq had not capitulated.[58] As Schwarzkopf saw it, his job was to get back coalition prisoners and dead bodies, establish clear lines separating forces, and locate minefields. He did not believe he was responsible for negotiating a peace agreement with the Iraqi government. Still, even 'purely military' matters have political ramifications, but Schwarzkopf lacked the legal and diplomatic support he needed to reach what was in effect a peace settlement. In fact, he acted with little guidance from Washington. While the Office of the Secretary of Defense drafted guidelines for the talks, the Joint Chiefs of Staff rebuffed them.[59]

Schwarzkopf's actions at Safwan further undermined US leverage over Iraq. At least in theory, the United States retained some coercive leverage over Baghdad through its occupation of thousands of miles of Iraqi territory and its ability to restart the war whenever it chose to do so. However, Schwarzkopf's statements to his Iraqi counterparts eroded both. He made it clear that the United States had no intention of changing Iraq's borders.[60] He also assured the Iraqi delegation that the United States planned to withdraw its forces as soon as possible.[61] These statements eliminated any opportunity for the United States to use the occupation of southern Iraq for leverage. Without consulting Khaled or Washington, Schwarzkopf allowed the Iraqi armed forces to fly helicopters over Iraqi territory, something that helped them crush the Shi'a rebellion in southern Iraq. The two sides signed no agreements, let alone articles of surrender. Khaled, for one, was disappointed that there was no formal document of surrender, which he believed might have helped remove Saddam.[62]

STRATEGIC OPTIONS

Supporters of the decision to halt the war at the 100-hour mark generally cite five arguments in support of their position. First, they contend that by 28 February the coalition had achieved its objectives. They argue that after 100 hours of ground combat, Iraq had been forced to withdraw from Kuwait, the Kuwaiti government was ready to be restored, Saddam's ability to threaten the region had been greatly curtailed, and the safety and security of Americans abroad was assured. James Baker reflects the perception, rather than the reality, of the situation when he writes that, by the ceasefire, 'the vast bulk of Iraq's military machine, including most of its nuclear, chemical, and biological weapons programs, was destroyed. Our core political and war aims having been achieved, there was literally no reason to contemplate sending our forces further north.'[63] Of note is the fact that the United States did not even discover, let alone destroy, the vast majority of Iraqi nuclear, biological and chemical programs until the establishment of the United Nations Special Commission on Iraq after the war. More fundamentally, such a view confuses the operational center of gravity – the Iraqi army in Kuwait – with the strategic center of gravity – Saddam and his regime.

Second, supporters argue that continuing the ground campaign would have changed the nature of the war. Had coalition forces invaded Iraq, they potentially could have faced determined resistance by the Iraqis. Soldiers who had been unwilling to defend Kuwait would have been more determined in defending their own homes. Bush and his advisors worried that invading Iraq would be tantamount to 'assigning young soldiers to a fruitless hunt for a securely entrenched dictator and condemning them to fight in what would be an unwinnable urban guerrilla war'.[64] Such a view ignores the fact that by 1 March the Iraqi army in Kuwait had been broken. There were few effective Iraqi units between the coalition and Baghdad.

Third, supporters argue that, if the coalition had continued the war and marched on Baghdad, Iraq might have escalated to the use of chemical or biological weapons. Fourth, a continuation of the war could have led to the collapse of Iraq. Analysts in the US intelligence community worried that Iraq might collapse into three enclaves – the Kurds in the north, the Sunni Moslems in the central region around Baghdad, and the Shi'a Moslems in the south.[65] They were particularly concerned that Iran would exploit the disorder to increase its influence in southern Iraq.

The record of Iraq's behavior since the Gulf War contradicts this view. Saddam Hussein's Ba'th regime – dominated by the country's minority Sunni population – brutally suppressed Shi'a uprisings in the south and the Kurds in the north, despite just having lost a war. In the decade following the conflict, Saddam was able to rule Iraq with an iron fist, even given the limitations to Iraqi sovereignty imposed by the United Nations. Thus in retrospect the assumption that Iraq was ready to fall apart seems at best questionable.

Finally, supporters of the decision to halt the ground war after 100 hours argue that the continuation of the war would have split the multi-national coalition. Had we tried to install a new Iraqi government, they argue, the Arab public would likely have turned against us. That regime would have been branded from the start as an American puppet, and we would have acquired a long-term commitment to keep propping it up.[66] In fact, the region's moderate Arab governments needed Saddam out of power even more than the United States did, even if they could not say so in public.

Clearly, a march on Baghdad would have entailed such risks. It could have changed the nature of the war. It could have led to escalation. And it could have fractured the coalition. But there were many options between stopping the war at the 100-hour mark or going all the way to Baghdad. The United States had at least four options to continue pressuring Saddam, each of which was considered at some level within the US government during the war. Each offered the prospect of bringing home to the government in Baghdad the reality that it had lost the war and weakening Saddam's hold on power. Each also held out the possibility of so discrediting Saddam that he would be overthrown in favor of a regime capable of reaching a *modus vivendi* with the coalition.

Continue the Ground War

First, the United States could have continued the ground war until its forces had completely enveloped the Republican Guard. The Republican Guard represented Iraq's operational center of gravity, a fact that CENTCOM had recognized early in Operation Desert Shield. It was not only Iraq's most effective fighting force, but also one of the pillars of Saddam Hussein's regime. By exerting pressure on the guards, the United States would have gained additional leverage. When the ceasefire was announced, VII and XVIII Corps were on the verge of trapping the remainder of the Republican Guard in the theater. Rather than calling a halt to hostilities and then opening negotiations with Baghdad, Washington should have called for talks while continuing to use military operations to pressure Saddam.

Coalition forces would have been able to completely encircle and destroy the Republican Guards within another day or so. While supporters of the decision to halt the war have argued that US forces were tired and overstretched by 28 February,[67] the US army's official study of the Gulf War concluded that CENTCOM forces could have sustained operations long enough to complete the mission.[68] As General Franks later wrote, 'I cannot help but think that the end of the war might have turned out differently if they had been able to continue forward and we could have finalized the VII Corps–XVIII Corps coordinated final attack.'[69] Similarly, critics argue that encircling Iraqi forces retreating on Basra would have led to high American casualties and a wholesale slaughter of Iraqis.[70] Commanders on the scene, however, felt otherwise. They believed that a drive to the Basra canal would have bypassed the bulk of the remaining Iraqi forces and would have incurred few American casualties.[71]

The participants leave little doubt that Bush would have been willing to authorize the continuation of the war. Powell has written that 'there is no doubt in my mind that if Norm or I had the slightest reservation about stopping now, the President would have given us all the time we needed'.[72] Unfortunately, by leaving the decision to halt the war to his commanders, Bush gave the military the latitude to make a decision that was essentially political in character.

Powell's failure to understand the intimate relationship between operational success and victory is evident in the following passage from his memoirs:

> It is true that more tanks and Republican Guard troops escaped from Kuwait than we expected. And yes we could have taken another day or two to close that escape hatch … But it would not [have] made a bit of difference in Saddam's future conduct.[73]

In fact, there is reason to believe that encircling and annihilating the Republican Guard *would* have affected Saddam's attitude toward the coalition and his grip on power. At the very least, it is a subject that deserved more discussion than it received.

Feint Toward Baghdad

A second option would have been for coalition forces to make a feint toward Baghdad. In the estimation of General Sir Peter de la Billière, the commander of British forces in the Gulf, coalition forces could have made it to Baghdad in another day and a half and would have met little resistance along the way.[74] Even if the United States did not intend to march on the Iraqi capital, Washington could have used the threat of continued ground operations to bring home the magnitude of the disaster that

Saddam had brought down on Iraq. There was certainly no need to remove the threat of continued offensive operations by halting prior to opening negotiations. Nor should Schwarzkopf have reassured the Iraqis at Safwan that the United States did not plan on changing Iraq's borders. Instead, Washington should have continued to pressure Saddam until he publicly conceded or left power.

Occupy Iraqi Oilfields

Third, coalition forces could have occupied Iraqi territory for additional bargaining leverage. Oil was – and is – Iraq's top export, and a dispute over oil production had been one of the main causes of the war. At the close of the war, coalition ground forces occupied thousands of square miles of southern Iraq, including the Rumaila oil fields that sit astride the Iraqi–Kuwaiti border. Former British Prime Minister Margaret Thatcher believed that coalition forces should have occupied the oil fields until the demands upon Iraq had fully been met.[75] Such a move would arguably have given the coalition significant leverage over Iraq. However, soldiers and statesmen in Washington had no stomach for such a move. As James Baker put it, 'There was no sentiment at senior levels of the US government for occupying even part of Iraq. In addition, our military was adamantly opposed.'[76]

Force Saddam to Assume Burden of Defeat

Finally, the coalition could have done more to force Saddam to shoulder the responsibility for his actions. While the United States government called upon him 'personally and publicly' to accept responsibility for the war, it never pressed Iraq on this point. Khaled argued that the Iraqis should at least send a member of the Revolutionary Command Council to Safwan to link Saddam directly to Iraq's defeat. He also favored keeping military pressure on Saddam until he complied fully with coalition demands.[77] There were some in the Bush administration who discussed forcing Saddam personally to accept the terms of Iraqi defeat at Safwan, and thus responsibility for such a devastating defeat. However, Bush and his advisors could not figure out what to do if he refused. They felt that they would be left with the option of either continuing the war until he capitulated, or backing down. They feared that a continuation of the war would have split the coalition. As a result, they allowed Saddam to avoid personal surrender and send two generals to Safwan.[78]

CONCLUSION

As the Gulf War shows, determining when to end a war requires acute political and strategic judgement, particularly when decision-makers are operating under pressure without the benefit of accurate information. Exceeding the culminating point of victory can sap domestic and international support for military action while strengthening the adversary's resolve. By contrast, halting too soon can yield an incomplete victory and leave in place a foe that is weakened but unchastened. Even though the Bush administration did an outstanding job of planning and conducting the Gulf War, it encountered considerable difficulty determining when to end it.

The decision to end the Gulf War after 100 hours of ground combat was taken in haste without an adequate consideration of how to translate the lopsided battlefield outcome of the war into a durable postwar settlement. The US government ignored the need to exert continuing pressure upon Saddam and his regime to live up to the pledges it made to the United Nations. The declaration of a unilateral halt to the war, coupled with Schwarzkopf's statements during his briefing on 27 February, and at Safwan, virtually eliminated the possibility that the United States would restart the war.

The war provides a concrete example of the persistence of friction on the modern battlefield. US forces in the Gulf War possessed a better picture of the battlefield than their counterparts in previous (and, given the nature of the theater, subsequent) conflicts. Yet a vast array of modern sensors and communication systems was unable to banish the fog of war from the battlefield.[79] At the operational level, it is clear that Schwarzkopf lost track of the position of his forces and Iraqi troops at a critical point in the battle. As a result, he believed that coalition forces had sealed off the escape routes from Kuwait when they had not.

The war represents a failure at a broader level as well. It is clear that decision-makers in Washington did not understand Saddam and the nature of his regime. They devoted little attention to understanding him and developing methods to exert pressure on him. They assumed that his grip on power was weak and that the Iraqi state was fragile. Neither proved to be true. This misunderstanding circumscribed the ability of the United States to translate its battlefield success into strategic leverage.

If one is looking for scapegoats, there is plenty of blame to go around. Schwarzkopf was clearly guilty of practicing 'chateau generalship'.[80] By the closing stages of the ground war, he had lost track of his forces on the battlefield. He and his staff gave their military and civilian superiors the false impression that US forces had accomplished their mission when they had not, a misperception that he reinforced in his news conference on the evening of 27 February. At that briefing and again at Safwan, he made statements that limited the range of strategic options available to his civilian superiors. Powell also deserves a share of the blame. He frequently gave advice that was more political than military. As the conduit between Schwarzkopf and the national leadership, he tended to substitute his own views for the theater commander's judgement.

In the end, however, the military was only partially to blame for the decision to halt the Gulf War after 100 hours of ground combat. The nation's civilian leadership failed to think through the end of the war. As George Bush and Brent Scowcroft later admitted, 'The end of effective Iraqi resistance came with a rapidity which surprised us all, and we were perhaps psychologically unprepared for the sudden transition from fighting to peacemaking.'[81]

The civilian leadership proved to be too deferential to Powell and Schwarzkopf. Bush was determined to avoid a replay of Vietnam, during which Lyndon Johnson and his advisors selected individual targets for air attack. In the process of giving the military considerable latitude for waging war, he and his advisors failed to give the military situation the type of scrutiny it required. The civilian leadership allowed the decision to end the war to be governed by purely military considerations such as the expulsion of Iraqi forces from Kuwait. In fact, the most important goal was political: the need to create a stable postwar situation in the Gulf. Soldiers in general, and the US armed forces in particular, tend to confuse operational success with victory. The military was qualified to determine when the Iraqi army had been expelled from Kuwait. It was also competent to advise the national leadership as to the level of damage that would render Iraqi units ineffective militarily. However, determining the military preconditions for stability in the Gulf was ultimately a political judgement. Yet Bush's advisors were virtually silent on this subject. Secretary of State Baker, who was responsible for American foreign policy, offered little advice during the meetings to discuss whether it was time to end the war. In the event, battlefield commanders were allowed to improvise decisions that should have been made at the highest political levels.

Because of the failure to compel Saddam Hussein to 'do our will' at the end of the Gulf War, Iraq remains a topic not only of historical interest but also of current concern. The United States has taken up a long-term presence in the Gulf, one that cannot help but cause friction with US friends in the region. Saddam, for his part, sees the outcome of the Gulf War as a transitory evil, and may very well seek a remedy at some later date. Thus ten years on, the aim of stability in the Persian Gulf remains as illusory as ever.

NOTES

The author would like to thank Michael I. Handel, Timothy D. Hoyt, Efraim Inbar and Andrew Parasiliti for their helpful comments on earlier drafts of this paper.

1. Colin Powell, with Joseph E. Persico, *My American Journey* (New York: Random House, 1995), p. 519.
2. Basil H. Liddell-Hart, *Strategy* (New York: Praeger, 1967), p. 351.
3. Carl von Clausewitz, *On War*, ed. and trans. Michael Howard and Peter Paret (Princeton, NJ: Princeton University Press, 1976), p. 75.

4. For an insightful discussion, see Michael I. Handel, *Masters of War: Classical Strategic Thought* (London: Frank Cass, 2001), p. 203.
5. Clausewitz, *On War*, p. 69.
6. Fred Charles Iklé, *Every War Must End* (New York: Columbia University Press, 1991), p. 17.
7. Indeed, in some cases, such as guerrilla warfare, they may not even be necessary to achieve victory.
8. Michael Howard, 'When are Wars Decisive?', *Survival*, 41, 1 (Spring 1999), p. 132; Brian Bond, *The Pursuit of Victory: From Napoleon to Saddam Hussein* (Oxford: Oxford University Press, 1996), pp. 5, 202.
9. Clausewitz, *On War*, p. 92. See also Handel, *Masters of War*, Chap. 14.
10. Clausewitz, *On War*, p. 92. For a detailed discussion of the rational calculus of war, see Handel, *Masters of War*, Chap. 7.
11. Michael I. Handel, 'The Problem of War Termination', in Michael I. Handel, *War, Strategy, and Intelligence* (London: Frank Cass, 1989), pp. 471–3; Iklé, *Every War Must End*, p. 15. See also Richard K. Betts, 'Is Strategy an Illusion?', *International Security*, 25, 2 (Fall 2000), pp. 5–50.
12. Robert McQuie, 'Battle Outcomes: Casualty Rates as a Measure of Defeat', *Army*, 37 (November 1987), p. 33.
13. See also Col. Theodore L. Gatchel, USMC, 'Can a Battle Be Lost in the Mind of the Commander?', *Naval War College Review*, 38, 1 (January–February 1985).
14. Barry R. Posen, 'The War for Kosovo: Serbia's Political–Military Strategy', *International Security*, 24, 4 (Spring 2000), pp. 39–84.
15. Clausewitz, *On War*, p. 92; Handel, *Masters of War*, p. 78.
16. National Security Directive 54, 'Responding to Iraqi Aggression in the Gulf', 15 January 1991, www.gwu.edu/~nsarchiv/NSAEBB/NSAEBB39.
17. Richard M. Swain, '*Lucky War': Third Army in Desert Storm* (Ft Leavenworth, KS: US Army Command and General Staff College Press, 1997), p. 250.
18. George Bush and Brent Scowcroft, *A World Transformed* (New York: Knopf, 1998), p. 481.
19. Ibid., p. 482.
20. Ibid., p. 483.
21. Michael R. Gordon and Bernard E. Trainor, *The Generals' War* (Boston, MA: Little, Brown, 1995), p. 404.
22. Bush and Scowcroft, *A World Transformed*, p. 484.
23. Ibid.
24. Gen. Robert H. Scales, *Certain Victory: The US Army in the Gulf War* (Ft Leavenworth, KS: US Army Command and General Staff College Press, 1994), pp. 308–9. See also Tom Clancy, with Gen. Fred Franks, Jr (ret.), *Into the Storm: On the Ground in Iraq* (New York: G.P. Putnam, 1997), p. 424.
25. Gordon and Trainor, *The Generals' War*, p. 404; Scales, *Certain Victory*, p. 308.
26. Powell, *My American Journey*, pp. 521–2; Rick Atkinson, *Crusade: The Untold Story of the Persian Gulf War* (New York: Houghton Mifflin, 1993), p. 471.
27. Gordon and Trainor, *The Generals' War*, p. 418.
28. Handel, *Masters of War*, Chap. 13.
29. Atkinson, *Crusade*, p. 470; Gordon and Trainor, *The Generals' War*, p. 424.
30. Bush and Scowcroft, *A World Transformed*, p. 484.
31. Clausewitz, *On War*, p. 84.
32. Gordon and Trainor, *The Generals' War*, p. 418; Powell, *My American Journey*, p. 521; Bush and Scowcroft, *A World Transformed*, pp. 485–6; H. Norman Schwarzkopf, with Peter Petre, *It Doesn't Take a Hero* (New York: Bantam, 1992), pp. 469–70. On Schwarzkopf's tendency to yield to Powell, see Gordon and Trainor, *The Generals' War*, p. 423.
33. Quoted in Lawrence E. Cline, 'Defending the End: Decision Making in Terminating the Persian Gulf War', *Comparative Strategy*, 17, 4 (October–December

1998), p. 368; Powell, *My American Journey*, p. 524.
34. Gordon and Trainor, *The Generals' War*, p. 419; Schwarzkopf, *It Doesn't Take a Hero*, p. 470.
35. Franks, *Into the Storm*, p. 443. That afternoon, Franks had told Yeosock that his forces would require another day to complete their mission. However, Yeosock did not consult with Franks on the progress of VII Corps' advance thereafter. See ibid., p. 428.
36. Gordon and Trainor, *The Generals' War*, pp. 419, 425.
37. Ibid., p. 415.
38. Michael Sterner, 'Closing the Gate: The Persian Gulf War Revisited', *Current History*, 96, 606 (January 1997), p. 16.
39. Gordon and Trainor, *The Generals' War*, pp. 424, 425.
40. Clausewitz, *On War*, pp. 469–70.
41. Bush and Scowcroft, *A World Transformed*, pp. 486–7.
42. James A. Baker, III, *The Politics of Diplomacy: Revolution, War and Peace, 1989–1992* (New York: G.P. Putnam, 1995), p. 437.
43. Bush and Scowcroft, *A World Transformed*, pp. 487–8.
44. Swain, 'Lucky War', p. 285; Schwarzkopf, *It Doesn't Take a Hero*, pp. 470–1.
45. Gordon and Trainor, *The Generals' War*, p. 423.
46. Ibid., p. 426.
47. Powell, *My American Journey*, p. 523.
48. Gordon and Trainor, *The Generals' War*, p. 424.
49. Gen. Khaled bin Sultan, with Patrick Seale, *Desert Warrior: A Personal View of the Gulf War by the Joint Forces Commander* (New York: Harper Collins, 1995), p. 412; Gordon and Trainor, *The Generals' War*, p. 429.
50. Interview with Gen. Wafiq al-Samarrai, Head of Iraqi Military Intelligence, www.pbs.org/wgbh/pages/frontline/gulf/oral/summarai/1.html (accessed 26 April 2000).
51. Ibid.
52. Ibid.
53. Quoted in Lawrence Freedman and Efraim Karsh, *The Gulf Conflict 1990–1991: Diplomacy and War in the New World Order* (Princeton, NJ: Princeton University Press, 1993), p. 410.
54. Al-Samarrai interview.
55. Khaled bin Sultan, *Desert Warrior*, p. 422.
56. Ibid., p. 426.
57. Ibid., p. 424.
58. Rick Francona, *Ally to Adversary: An Eyewitness Account of Iraq's Fall from Grace* (Annapolis, MD: Naval Institute Press, 1999), p. 142.
59. Gordon and Trainor, *The Generals' War*, p. 444; Schwarzkopf, *It Doesn't Take a Hero*, p. 479.
60. Khaled bin Sultan, *Desert Warrior*, p. 435.
61. Gordon and Trainor, *The Generals' War*, p. 447.
62. Khaled bin Sultan, *Desert Warrior*, p. 426.
63. Baker, *The Politics of Diplomacy*, p. 437.
64. Bush and Scowcroft, *A World Transformed*, p. 464.
65. Francona, *Ally to Adversary*, p. 138.
66. Baker, *The Politics of Diplomacy*, p. 437; Bush and Scowcroft, *A World Transformed*, p. 489; Khaled bin Sultan, *Desert Warrior*, p. 426; Powell, *My American Journey*, p. 526.
67. Cline, 'Defending the End', p. 368.
68. Scales, *Certain Victory*, p. 314.
69. Franks, *Into the Storm*, p. 409.
70. Sterner, 'Closing the Gate', p. 16.
71. Gordon and Trainor, *The Generals' War*, p. 425.

72. Powell, My American Journey, p. 522.
73. Ibid., p. 526.
74. Gen. Sir Peter de la Billière, Storm Command: A Personal Account of the Gulf War (London: Harper Collins, 1992), p. 304.
75. Gordon and Trainor, The Generals' War, pp. 413, 447.
76. Baker, The Politics of Diplomacy, p. 438.
77. Khaled bin Sultan, Desert Warrior, pp. 423, 425.
78. Bush and Scowcroft, A World Transformed, p. 490.
79. For an excellent discussion of this, see Barry D. Watts, Clausewitzian Friction and Future War, McNair Paper 52 (Washington, DC: National Defense University Press, 1996).
80. Swain, 'Lucky War', p. 250.
81. Bush and Scowcroft, A World Transformed, p. 488.

7

'Splendid Little War': America's Persian Gulf Adventure Ten Years On

ANDREW J. BACEVICH

I

'Nearly a decade after its conclusion,' observes Frank Rich of the *New York Times*, 'the Persian Gulf War is already looking like a footnote to American history.'[1] Rich's appraisal of Operation Desert Storm and the events surrounding it manages to be at once accurate and yet massively wrong.

Rich is certainly correct in the sense that, ten years on, the war no longer appears as it did in 1990 and 1991: a colossal feat of arms, a courageous and adeptly executed stroke of statesmanship, and a decisive response to aggression that laid the basis for a new international order. The 'official' view of the war, energetically promoted by senior US officials and military officers and, at least for a time, echoed and amplified by an exultant national media, has become obsolete.

In outline, that official story was simplicity itself: unprovoked and dastardly aggression, a small peace-loving nation snuffed out of existence, a line drawn in the sand, a swift and certain response by the United States that mobilizes the international community to put things right. The outcome too was unambiguous. Speaking from the Oval Office on 28 February 1991 as he announced the suspension of combat operations, President George Bush left no room for doubt that the United

States had achieved precisely the outcome that it had sought: 'Kuwait is liberated. Iraq's army is defeated. Our military objectives are met.'[2] Characterizing his confrontation with Saddam Hussein's army, General Norman Schwarzkopf used more colorful language to make the same point.[3]

In the war's immediate aftermath, America's desert victory seemed not only decisive but without precedent in the annals of military history. Such a stunning achievement fueled expectations that Desert Storm would pay dividends extending far beyond the military sphere. These expectations – even more than the action on the battlefield – persuaded Americans that the war marked a momentous turning-point. In a stunning riposte to critics who throughout the 1980s had argued that the USA had slipped into a period of irreversible decline, the Persian Gulf War announced emphatically that America was back and on top.

Thus, in a single stroke, the war seemingly healed psychic wounds that had festered for a generation. Reflecting the views of many professional officers, General Colin Powell, chairman of the Joint Chiefs of Staff, believed that the demons of the Vietnam War had at long last been exorcised. Thanks to Operation Desert Storm, he wrote, 'the American people fell in love again with their armed forces'.[4] Indeed, references to 'the troops' – a phrase to which politicians, pundits and network anchors all took a sudden liking – conveyed a not-so-subtle shift in attitude toward soldiers, suggesting a level of empathy, respect and even affection that had been absent and even unimaginable since the late 1960s.

Bush himself proclaimed famously that with its victory in the Persian Gulf the United States had at long last kicked the so-called Vietnam Syndrome.[5] That did not mean that the President welcomed the prospect of more such military adventures. If anything, the reverse was true: its military power unshackled, the United States would henceforth find itself employing force *less* frequently. 'I think because of what has happened, we won't have to use US forces around the world,' Bush predicted during his first postwar press conference. 'I think when we say something that is objectively correct ... people are going to listen.'[6]

To the President and his advisors, the vivid demonstration of US military prowess in the Gulf had put paid to lingering doubts about American credibility. Looking past the war itself, that credibility endowed the United States with a unique opportunity – not only to prevent the recurrence of aggression but also to lay the foundation for what Bush called a new world order. American power would shape that order. American power would also guarantee the United States a pre-eminent place in that order. America would 'reach out to the rest of the world', Bush and National Security Advisor Brent Scowcroft wrote, but in doing so would 'keep the strings of control tightly in our hands'.[7]

This view accorded precisely with the Pentagon's own preferences. Cherishing their newly restored prestige, American military leaders were by no means eager to put it at risk. Thus, they touted the Gulf War not simply as a singular victory but as a paradigmatic event, a conflict that revealed the future of war and outlined the proper role of US military power. Powell and his fellow generals rushed to codify the war's key 'lessons'. Clearly stated objectives related to vital national interests, the employment of overwhelming force and superior technology, commanders insulated from political meddling, a pre-designated 'exit strategy' – these had produced a brief, decisive campaign fought according to the norms of conventional warfare, concluded at modest cost and without moral complications. If the generals got their way, standing ready to conduct future Desert Storms would henceforth define the US military's central purpose.

Finally, the war also seemingly had large implications for domestic politics – although whether those implications were cause for celebration or despondency depended on one's partisan affiliation. In the war's immediate aftermath, Bush's approval ratings rocketed above 90 per cent. In the eyes of most experts, the President's adept handling of the Persian Gulf crisis all but guaranteed his election to a second term.

II

Subsequent events have not dealt kindly with these expectations. Indeed, the 1992 presidential election – when Americans handed the architect of victory in the Gulf his walking papers – hinted that the war's actual legacy would be different from that originally advertised. In fact, the fruits of victory turned out to be other than expected. Bill Clinton's elevation to the office of Commander-in-Chief was only one among several surprises.

For starters, America's love affair with the troops turned out to be more of an infatuation than a lasting commitment. A series of embarrassing scandals – beginning just months after Desert Storm with the US navy's infamous Tailhook convention in 1991 – thrust the military into the center of the ongoing *Kulturkampf*. Rather than basking contentedly in the glow of victory, military institutions found themselves pilloried for being out of step with enlightened attitudes on such matters as gender and sexual orientation. In early 1993, the generals embroiled themselves in a nasty public confrontation with their new commander-in-chief over the question of whether or not gays should serve openly in the military. In this particular instance, the top brass prevailed. But 'don't ask, don't tell' would prove to be a Pyrrhic victory.

The real story of military policy in the 1990s was the transformation of the armed services from bastions of masculinity (an increasingly suspect quality) into institutions that were accommodating to women and also 'family-friendly'. The result was a major advance in the crusade for absolute gender equality, secured by watering down or simply discarding traditional notions of military culture and unit cohesion. By the decade's end, Americans took it as a matter of course that female fighter pilots were flying strike missions over Iraq and that a terrorist attack on an American warship found female sailors among the dead and wounded.

As the military became increasingly feminized, young American men evinced a dwindling inclination to serve. The Pentagon insisted that the two developments were unrelated. Although the active military shrunk by a third in overall size during the decade following the Gulf War, the services found themselves by the end of the 1990s increasingly hard pressed to keep the ranks full. Military leaders attributed the problem to a booming economy – the private sector offered a better deal. Their solution was to improve pay and benefits, to deploy additional platoons of recruiters and to redouble their efforts to market their 'product'. In an effort to burnish its drab image, the US army, the most hard-pressed of the services, even adopted new headgear – a beret. With less fanfare, each service also began to relax its enlistment standards.

Similarly, when it came to the actual use of military power, Bush's expectations (and Powell's hope) that the United States would only rarely employ force did not materialize. The outcome of the Gulf War – and, more significantly, the outcome of the Cold War – created conditions more conducive to disorder than order, confronting both Bush and his successor with situations that each would view as intolerable. Inaction would undermine US claims to global leadership and risked the revival of isolationist habits. It was imperative that the United States remain engaged. As a result, the decade following victory in the Gulf became a period of unprecedented American military activism.

The motives for intervention varied as widely as the particular circumstances on the ground. In 1991, Bush sent US troops into northern Iraq to protect Kurdish refugees fleeing from Saddam Hussein. Following his electoral defeat in 1992, he tasked the military to undertake a major humanitarian effort in Somalia, attempting to bring order to a failed state and aid to a people facing mass starvation. Not to be outdone, Bill Clinton ordered the military occupation of Haiti to remove a military junta from power and to 'restore' democracy. Moved by the horrors of ethnic cleansing, Clinton bombed and occupied Bosnia. Largely unmoved by genocide, he intervened in Rwanda after the slaughter there had largely run its course. Determined to prevent NATO from being discredited, he fought a substantial war for Kosovo, providing Slobodan Milosevic with a pretext for renewed ethnic cleansing, which NATO's military action did little to arrest. In lesser actions, President Clinton employed cruise missiles to retaliate (ineffectually) against Saddam Hussein for allegedly plotting to assassinate his predecessor and against Usama Bin Laden for terrorist attacks on two US embassies in Africa in 1998. As the impeachment crisis loomed at the end of 1998, the President renewed hostilities against Iraq, a brief air offensive known as Operation Desert Fox in December 1998 giving way to a persistent but desultory bombing campaign that sputtered on until the very end of his presidency.

These operations shared one common feature: each one violated the terms of the so-called Powell Doctrine regarding the use of force. The 'end-state' sought by military action was seldom clearly defined and was often modified at mid-course. (In Somalia, the mission changed from feeding the starving to waging war against Somali warlords.) More often than not, intervention led not to a prompt and decisive outcome but to open-ended commitments. (President Clinton sent US peacekeepers into Bosnia in 1995 promising to withdraw them in a year; over five years later when Clinton left office GIs were still garrisoning the Balkans.) In contrast to Powell's preference for using overwhelming force, expending military power in discrete increments – to punish, to signal resolve or to influence behavior – became the norm. (Operation Allied Force in 1999 proceeded on the illusory assumption that a three- or four-day demonstration of air power would persuade Slobodan Milosevic to submit to NATO's will.) Nor were American soldiers able to steer clear of the moral complications that went hand in hand with these untidy conflicts. (The United States and NATO won in Kosovo by bringing the war home to the Serb population, an uncomfortable reality from which some sought to escape by proposing to waive the principle of non-combatant immunity.)[8]

In other words, the events that dashed President Bush's dreams of a new world order also rendered the Powell Doctrine obsolete and demolished expectations that the Persian Gulf War might provide a template for the planning and execution of future US military operations. By the fall of 2000, when a bomb-laden rubber boat rendered a billion-dollar US navy destroyer *hors de combat* and killed 17 Americans, the notion that the mere possession of superior military technology and know-how provided the United States with the ultimate trump card rang hollow.

III

Judged in terms of predictions and expectations voiced in its immediate aftermath, the Persian Gulf War does seem destined to end up as little more than a historical afterthought. Unburdening the war of those inflated expectations, however, makes it possible to place the war in a different context, one that yields an altogether different perspective on the actual legacy of Desert Storm. If lacking the resplendence that in 1991 seemed the war's proper birthright, that legacy promises to be significant and enduring.

Reaching a fair evaluation of the war's significance requires first that Americans situate it correctly in the grand narrative of US military history. In that regard, Desert Storm clearly does not rank with military enterprises such as the Civil War or World War II. Nor does the abbreviated campaign in the desert bear comparison with the other twentieth-century conflicts such as World War I, Korea or Vietnam. Rather, the most appropriate comparison is with that other 'splendid little war', the Spanish–American War of 1898. Norman Schwarzkopf's triumph over the obsolete army of Saddam Hussein ranks on a par with Admiral Dewey's fabled triumph over an antiquated Spanish naval squadron at Manila Bay. Both qualify as genuine military victories. But the true measure of each is not the economy and dispatch with which US forces vanquished their adversary but the entirely unforeseen, and largely problematic, consequences to which each victory gave rise.

Viewed in retrospect, the Spanish–American War – not just Dewey at Manila Bay but Teddy Roosevelt leading the charge up San Juan Hill and General Nelson Miles 'liberating' Puerto Rico – was a trivial military episode. That judgement notwithstanding, the war also marked a profound turning-point in US history. The brief conflict with Spain ended any compunction that Americans may have felt about the feasibility or propriety of imposing their own norms and values on others. With this war, the nation enthusiastically shouldered its share of the White Man's Burden, presiding thereafter over colonies and client states in the Caribbean and the Pacific. The war saddled the

American military with new responsibilities to govern that empire and with one large nearly insoluble strategic problem – how to defend the Philippines, the largest of the Spanish possessions to which the United States laid claim. In short, it propelled the United States into the ranks of great powers. Notable features of the century that followed – none of them even remotely visible when William McKinley set out to free Cubans from the yoke of Spanish oppression – all derive to a greater or lesser extent from the events of 1898. These would include an ugly campaign to pacify the Philippines, a pattern of repetitive military intervention in the Caribbean, America's tortured relationship with Cuba, and three bloody Asian wars fought in three decades.

A similar case can be made with regard to the Persian Gulf War, which, however puny in a strictly military sense, is giving birth to its own equally significant – and equally ambiguous – legacy. It is in this sense that inclinations to consign the war to footnote status are wide of the mark.

A preliminary assessment of that legacy suggests that it consists of at least four distinct elements. First, the Gulf War transformed American views regarding armed conflict – the nature of war, the determinants of success, and expectations of when and how US forces should intervene.

Operation Desert Storm seemingly reversed one of the principal lessons of Vietnam, namely that excessive reliance on technology in war offers a recipe for disaster. In the showdown with Iraq, technology proved to be crucial to success. In this context, technology meant *American* technology since other members of the coalition (with the partial exception of Great Britain) lagged far behind US forces. And above all, technology meant American *airpower*, since it was the effects of the bombing campaign preceding the brief ground offensive that provided the real 'story' of the Gulf War. After coalition airmen had isolated, weakened and demoralized Saddam Hussein's army, the actual liberation of Kuwait appeared to be hardly more than an afterthought.

With Operation Desert Storm, a century or more of industrial age warfare came to an end and a new era of information

156

age warfare beckoned – a style of warfare, it went without saying, to which the United States was uniquely attuned. In the information age, airpower promised to be for warfare a clean, economical and nearly painless remedy to a wide array of complaints.

Gone apparently were the days of slugfests, stalemates and bloodbaths. Gone too were the days when battlefield mishaps – a building erroneously bombed, an American soldier's life lost to friendly fire – could be ascribed to the fog and friction inherent in war. Such occurrences now became 'inexplicable errors' that demanded an explanation and accounting. The nostrums of the information age equate information to power. They dictate that the greater availability of information should eliminate uncertainty and enhance abilities to anticipate and control events. Even if the key piece of information becomes apparent only after the fact, someone – commander or pilot or analyst – 'should have known'.

Thus did the Persian Gulf War feed expectations of no-fault operations. The Pentagon itself encouraged such expectations, engaging in its own flights of fancy. Doctrine developed by the Joint Chiefs of Staff in the 1990s publicly committed US forces to harnessing technology to achieve what it called 'full spectrum dominance' – the capability to prevail, quickly and cheaply, in any and all forms of conflict.

This technological utopianism, in turn, has had two perverse effects. The first has been to persuade political elites that war can and ought to be virtually bloodless. The imperative of bloodless war will strike some as so bizarre that only a bona fide Washington insider (or techno-geek soldier) could take it seriously. But as the war for Kosovo demonstrated in 1999, such considerations now play a decisive effect in shaping US military operations. How else to explain a war allegedly fought for humanitarian purposes in which the commander-in-chief publicly renounces the use of ground troops and restricts combat aircraft to altitudes at which their efforts to protect the victims of persecution are necessarily ineffective?

Technological utopianism has also altered fundamentally the moral debate about war and the use of force. During the decades following Hiroshima, that debate centered on assessing the moral implications of nuclear war and nuclear deterrence – an agenda that put moral reasoning at the service of averting Armageddon. Since the Persian Gulf War, theologians and ethicists once openly skeptical of using force in all but the direst circumstances have evolved a far more expansive and accommodating view. This has been so much the case that in places remote from any tangible American interests – the Balkans and sub-Saharan Africa, for example – they now find that the United States has a positive obligation to intervene. As others have noted, more than a few doves have developed markedly hawkish tendencies.

The second element of the Gulf War's legacy is a new consensus about the relationship between military power and America's national identity. In the aftermath of Desert Storm, military pre-eminence, as never before, has become an integral part of that identity. The idea that the United States presides as the world's only superpower – an idea that the Persian Gulf War more than any other single event made manifest – has not only found favor with the great majority of Americans; most can no longer conceive of any alternative.

That US military spending now exceeds that of all the other so-called leading powers, whether long-standing friend or potential foe, *combined*, has been noted so frequently that it has lost all power to astonish. It has become non-controversial, an expression of the way things are meant to be and, by common consent, of the way they ought to remain. Yet in the presidential campaign of 2000, both the Democratic and Republican candidate agreed that the current level of defense spending – approaching $300 billion per year – is entirely inadequate. Tellingly, it was the nominee of the Democratic Party – ostensibly the seat of anti-military sentiment – who offered the more generous plan for boosting the Pentagon's budget. The campaign included no credible voices suggesting that the United States might already be spending *too much* on defense.

This consensus – forged at a moment when the actual threats to the nation's well-being were fewer than at any time since the 1920s – turns traditional American thinking about military power on its head. Although the Republic came into existence through a campaign of violence, the Founders did not view the experiment upon which they had embarked as an exercise in accruing military might. If anything, the reverse was true. By insulating America (politically but not commercially) from the Old World's preoccupations with war and militarism, they hoped to create in the New World something quite different.

Even during the Cold War, the notion had lingered that when it came to military matters America was indeed intended to be different. The United States government classified the Cold War as an 'emergency', as if implying that the level of mobilization that it entailed was only a temporary expedient. Even so, cold warriors with impeccable credentials – Dwight D. Eisenhower prominent among them – could be heard cautioning their fellow citizens to be wary of inadvertent militarism. The fall of the Berlin Wall might have offered the opportunity to reflect on Eisenhower's farewell address. But victory in the Gulf, seemingly demonstrating that military power was ineffably good, nipped any such inclination in the bud. When it came to Desert Storm, what was not to like?

Indeed, in some quarters America's easy win over Saddam Hussein inspired the belief that armed forces henceforth could do much more than simply 'fight and win the nation's wars'. Determined to demonstrate its continuing relevance in the absence of any plausible adversary, the Pentagon in the 1990s embraced an activist agenda, implementing a new 'strategy of engagement' whereby US forces devote their energies to 'shaping the international environment'. The idea, according to Secretary of Defense William Cohen, is:

> to shape people's opinions about us in ways that are favorable to us. To shape events that will affect our livelihood and our security. And we can do that when people see us, they see our power, they see our professionalism, they see our patriotism, and they say that's a country that we want to be with.[9]

American paratroopers jumping into Kazakhstan, US special forces training peacekeepers in Nigeria and counter-narcotics battalions in Colombia, and US warships stopping for fuel at the port of Aden – all these form part of an elaborate and ambitious effort to persuade others to 'be with' the world's pre-eminent power. Conceived in the Pentagon and directed by senior US military commanders, that effort proceeds quite openly, the particulars duly reported in the press. Few Americans pay it much attention. That the Pentagon's strategy arouses such little interest – suggesting that the general public has at least tacitly endorsed it – provides one measure of how comfortable Americans have become in wielding US military power a decade after the Persian Gulf War.

The third element of the Gulf War's legacy falls in the largely misunderstood and almost completely neglected province of civil–military relations. To the bulk of the officer corps, Desert Storm served to validate the Powell Doctrine. Put another way, it affirmed the military nostalgia that had taken root in the aftermath of Vietnam – the yearning to restore the concept of self-contained, decisive conventional war conducted by autonomous, self-governing military elites. Yet paradoxically, the actual result of Desert Storm has been to seal the demise of that concept. In the aftermath of the Persian Gulf War, the boundaries between war and peace, soldiers and civilians, combatants and non-combatants, the military and the political sphere have become more difficult than ever to discern. In some instances, those boundaries have all but disappeared.

Operation Allied Force – the American-led war for Kosovo in 1999 – provides the fullest expression to date of these tendencies. Over the course of an 11-week campaign, the Clinton administration never budged from its insistence that the military action in progress did not really constitute a war. As the bombing of Serbia intensified, it became unmistakably clear that the United States and its NATO partners assigned greater priority to protecting the lives of their own professional soldiers than either to aiding the victims of ethnic cleansing or to avoiding non-combatant casualties. When NATO ultimately prevailed, it did so by making war not on the Yugoslav army but on the Serb people.

The consequences of this blurring of civil–military distinctions extend well beyond the operational sphere. One effect has been to undermine the military profession's traditional claim that it be granted wide latitude in framing the policies that govern the armed forces. Simultaneously, however, in areas quite unrelated to the planning and conduct of combat operations, policy-makers have conferred on soldiers ever-greater authority. Thus, although the Persian Gulf War elevated military credibility to its highest point in memory, on policy matters touching even remotely on gender, senior officers today must conform to the politically correct position – that in war as in all other human endeavors gender is irrelevant. To express a contrary conviction is to imperil one's career, something which few generals and admirals are prone to do. Yet even while civilians dismiss the military's accumulated wisdom on matters relating to combat and unit cohesion, they are thrusting upon soldiers wider responsibilities for the formulation of foreign policy. In that regard, the four-star officers presiding over commands in Europe, the Middle East, Latin America and the Pacific have displaced the State Department as the ultimate arbiters of policy in those regions.

Thus, the ill-fated visit of the USS *Cole* to Aden in 2000 came not at the behest of some diplomatic functionary but on the order of General Anthony Zinni, the highly regarded US marine then serving as commander-in-chief (CINC) of United States Central Command, responsible for the Persian Gulf. Had Zinni expressed reservations about having a mixed-gender warship in his area of operations, he would, of course, have invited denunciation for commenting on matters beyond his purview. That in dispatching the *Cole* in pursuit of (in his words) 'more engagement' – part of a larger, misguided effort to befriend the Yemeni government – Zinni might be venturing into areas beyond his professional competence is something that no one would presume to ask.

Before his retirement, Zinni openly – and aptly – referred to the regional CINCs as 'proconsuls', an appropriately boundary-blurring term. For proconsuls fill an imperial mandate. Zinni is honest enough to acknowledge that in the post-Cold War world the CINC's function is quasi-imperial – recalling perhaps the role of General Douglas MacArthur presiding over occupied

Japan – even as Americans assure themselves that they neither possess an empire nor wish to acquire one. Projecting American power, maintaining order, enforcing norms of behavior, guarding American interests, the CINC/proconsul has become something more than a mere soldier. He straddles the worlds of politics, diplomacy and military affairs and moves easily between them. In so doing he has freed himself from the strictures that once defined the limits of soldierly prerogatives. Thus, upon stepping down as CINC, as the end of the 2000 presidential campaign neared, Zinni felt no compunction about immediately entering the partisan fray. He announced that the policies of the administration that he had served had all along been defective. With a clutch of other recently retired senior officers, he threw his support behind George W. Bush, an action intended to convey the impression that Bush was the military's preferred candidate.

Some critics have warned that no good could come from soldiers engaging in partisan politics. 'Nonsense' comes the response: when General Zinni endorses Bush or when General Schwarzkopf stumping the state of Florida denounces Democrats, they are merely exercising their constitutionally protected rights as citizens. In truth, the erosion of civil–military boundaries since the Persian Gulf War has emboldened officers to engage in such activities, reflecting an increasingly overt politicization of the officer corps. According to a time-honored tradition, to be an American military professional was to be apolitical. If in the past the odd general would toss his hat into the political arena – like Dwight D. Eisenhower in 1952 – his party affiliation came as a surprise and almost an afterthought. In the 1990s, with agenda-driven civilians intruding into military affairs and soldiers assuming the mantle of imperial proconsuls, that tradition went by the board. This too forms part of the Gulf War's legacy.

Finally and most importantly – if also most speculatively – the Gulf War powerfully influenced the way Americans have come to see the immediate past and the prospects of the immediate future. Occurring at the tail end of the twentieth century and just as the Cold War's final chapter was unfolding, victory in the desert seemingly affirmed that the years since the United States bounded onto the world stage in 1898 really *had* after all been the 'American Century'. Interpreted as an indisputable demonstration of American superiority, Operation Desert Storm once again made it plausible to believe that the rise of the United States to global dominance and the triumph of American values constituted the central theme of the century then coming to a close. In the collective public consciousness, the Persian Gulf War combined with the favorable conclusion of the Cold War proved that, despite two world wars, multiple episodes of genocide, and the mind-boggling criminality of totalitarianism, the twentieth century basically had turned out all right. In short, it enabled Americans to see contemporary history not as a chronicle of hubris, miscalculation and tragedy, but as a march of progress, its arc ever upward.

This perspective – however at odds with the post-modernism that pervades fashionable intellectual circles – makes possible the extraordinary expectations that Americans have carried into the new millennium. Bill Clinton has declared the United States to be 'the indispensable nation'. According to Madeleine Albright, the USA has become the 'organizing principal [sic]' of the global order.[10] 'If we have to use force, it is because we are America; we are the indispensable nation. We stand tall. We see further than other countries into the future.'[11] In sophisticated precincts such sentiments invite derision. But they play well in Peoria, according precisely with what most Americans wish to believe.

In 1898, a brief, one-sided war with Spain convinced Americans, certain that their intentions were benign, that destiny had endowed them with a unique responsibility and capacity to shoulder the task of uplifting 'little brown brother'. Large complications ensued. In 1991, a brief, one-sided war with Iraq persuaded Americans, confident that they had deciphered the secrets of history, that the rising tide of globalization points toward the ultimate triumph of American values. Yet a decade after the fact events in the Persian Gulf and its environs – the resurgence of Iraqi power under Saddam Hussein and the never-ending conflict between Israelis and Arabs – suggest that no end of complications await.

As Operation Desert Storm recedes into the distance, its splendor fades. But only now is the war's true significance beginning to come into view.

NOTES

1. Frank Rich, 'The Age of the Mediathon', *New York Times Magazine*, 29 October 2000.
2. George Bush and Brent Scowcroft, *A World Transformed* (New York: Knopf, 1998), p. 486.
3. H. Norman Schwarzkopf, *It Doesn't Take a Hero* (New York: Bantam, 1992).
4. Colin Powell, *My American Journey* (New York: Random House, 1995), p. 532.
5. Quoted in Stanley W. Cloud, 'Exorcising an Old Demon', *Newsweek*, 11 March 1991, p. 52.
6. President George Bush's press conference on the Persian Gulf conflict, 1 March 1991.
7. Bush and Scowcroft, *A World Transformed*, p. 491.
8. Col. Charles J. Dunlap, Jr, 'The End of Innocence: Rethinking Noncombatant Immunity in the Post-Kosovo Era', *Strategic Review*, 28 (Summer 2000), pp. 9–17.
9. William S. Cohen, 'US Must Remain Engaged in Post-Cold War Foreign Affairs', Foreign Policy Association, New York, 2 April 1998.
10. Madeleine Albright, 'Remarks at Tennessee State University', Nashville, TN, 19 February 1998.
11. Madeleine K. Albright, 'Interview on NBC-TV "The Today Show" with Matt Lauer', Columbus, OH, 19 February 1998.

Part V:

A Retrospective

8

The Middle East and the Gulf War: A Decade Later

EFRAIM KARSH

At the time of its occurrence, the 1991 Gulf War was widely viewed as the harbinger of a new international world order based on a resurgent spirit of collective solidarity. Those were the euphoric days attending the fall of the Berlin Wall and the rapid collapse of the east European communist regimes. There was much talk about the triumph of the West, the new world order and even the end of history. Regional conflicts were seen as almost condemned to extinction in the brave new world led by the 'only remaining superpower', the United States.

This of course is not how things have developed. While ridding the West of its foremost security concern of the past half-century, the collapse of the Eastern bloc and the disintegration of the Soviet Union have given rise to new international challenges which may prove no easier to handle. These range from a host of intractable ethnic and religious conflicts (for example, Yugoslavia, Rwanda, Somalia, Chechnya), to the leakage of nuclear know-how and technology to rogue states such as Iran and Iraq, to the substantial expansion of international terrorism, starkly demonstrated by the September 2001 attacks on New York and Washington. Moreover, as attested by America's difficulties to rally international support for its declared war against international terrorism, the forceful eviction of Iraq from Kuwait may prove to be the exception rather than the rule in the new world order, made possible by a unique period in international affairs. Had Saddam Hussein invaded Kuwait a few years earlier, such wide-ranging collaboration would have been inconceivable; had he taken a limited action against Kuwait, he might well have got away with it; had he been a minor dictator in a remote area, perhaps few would have bothered over the plight of his victim, or, more likely, a small punitive action might have redressed the situation.

As things stood, a regional superpower swallowing its small neighbor in one of the world's most sensitive areas seemed sufficiently alarming to orchestrate a diverse war coalition that would drive Iraq from Kuwait. Yet Saddam Hussein's remarkable survival after one of the most humiliating military defeats in contemporary history, as well as a decade of crippling sanctions, has qualified the whole episode. An enormous military effort had been undertaken, and yet there was Saddam, a decade later, thumbing his nose at the international community, having outlived all of the anti-Iraq coalition leaders, from George Bush to John Major, with his heroic stature in the Arab world hardly diminished and his hold on nuclear weapons closer than ever. This in turn has raised doubts about the war's long-term implications or even necessity: whether it has caused more harm than good or, indeed, whether it has made any difference at all.

Any serious discussion of these questions, however, must start from a consideration of the viable alternatives at the time and their implications, namely, was there a peaceful way to bring about Iraq's withdrawal from Kuwait, and, if not, would the Middle East have been a safer place with Kuwait remaining an Iraqi province?

There is little doubt that, had Iraq been allowed to retain the emirate, the Middle East would have been a far more dangerous place to live in. Not only would this have transformed Iraq into a regional superpower, armed with nuclear weapons and a huge arsenal of chemical and biological weapons, it might well have whetted Saddam's appetite for further conquests, thus making the world oil market virtually captive to the whims of a ruthless and unpredictable dictator.

To be sure, contrary to the American claims at the time, there is no evidence that Saddam ever intended to follow up the occupation of Kuwait with an invasion of Saudi Arabia. However, this is not to say that, had he been allowed to retain Kuwait, Saddam would not have developed wider ambitions, including the desire to have a far greater say in the world oil market. This is precisely why most Arab regimes, including the staunch Ba'thist Hafiz al-Asad, joined the American-led anti-Iraq coalition: not because of the US administration's persuasiveness or even the desire to gain access to American military and economic support, but because of the stark realization that, were Saddam to emerge from the crisis intact, let alone victorious, he would be impossible to coexist with. As the influential Saudi Ambassador to Washington, Prince Bandar Ibn Sultan, put it shortly after the invasion: 'He who eats Kuwait for breakfast is likely to ask for something else for lunch.'[1] Hence the Syrian objection to the American decision to end the war and their public advocacy of its continued prosecution until the toppling of Saddam.

Given the perceived importance of Kuwait's fabulous wealth for the survival of Saddam's personal rule, the only conceivable way to force the Iraqi dictator out of Kuwait was to persuade him that the costs of the emirate's continued occupation would by far exceed its potential gains. This, however, was easier said than done. Contrary to the received wisdom, Saddam is driven by neither a megalomaniac quest for regional hegemony, nor sentiments of pan-Arab solidarity, nor uncontrolled impetuosity. More than anything else, the origins of Saddam's conduct lie in his chronic political insecurity and the lengths to which this drove him. In the permanently beleaguered mind of Saddam, politics is a ceaseless struggle for survival, where the ultimate goal of staying alive and in power justifies all means. As he told a personal guest of his:

> I know that there are scores of people plotting to kill me and this is not difficult to understand. After all, did we not seize power by plotting against our predecessors? However, I am far cleverer than they are. I know they are conspiring to kill me long before they actually start planning to do it. This enables me to get them before they have the faintest chance of striking at me.[2]

This obsessive preoccupation with political survival drove Saddam to transform Iraq into one of the most repressive police states in today's world. During his years in power – both as *de facto* leader under President Ahmad Hasan al-Bakr since the early 1970s, and as President since July 1979 – Saddam totally subjected the ruling Ba'th Party to his will, sterilizing its governing institutions and reducing the national decision-making apparatus to one man, surrounded by a docile flock of close associates. Pre-empting any and all dissent through systematic purges (his ascent to the presidency, for example, was accompanied by the elimination of hundreds of party officials and military officers, some of whom were close friends and associates), he subordinated all domestic and foreign policies to one and only one goal: his political survival.

In September 1980 Saddam took Iraq to war against Iran, in an attempt to deflect the lethal threat posed to his personal rule by the revolutionary regime in Tehran, headed by the militant Ayatollah Ruhollah Khomeini. But when the guns fell silent in the summer of 1988, Saddam was confronted by yet another lethal threat which, in his perception, was bound sooner or later to lead to his undoing: an unprecedented economic plight generated by the Iran–Iraq War. As his pressures on the Kuwaitis to bail Iraq out of its predicament came to naught, Saddam decided to invade the emirate with the clear intention of incorporating its mammoth wealth into Iraq's state structures, so as to allow the recovery of the afflicted Iraqi economy and the launching of the ambitious reconstruction programs on which his personal rule hinged.

This state of affairs made Iraq's peaceful withdrawal from Kuwait virtually impossible. As far as Saddam was concerned, all carrots offered by the international coalition in return for such a withdrawal (for example, serious negotiations with the Kuwaitis on economic and territorial issues, progress on other regional disputes, etc.) could hardly address the dire economic straits that had driven him to invade Kuwait, and were then made worse by the anti-Iraq sanctions. Saddam knew that there would be no incentive for the Kuwaiti ruling family to concede anything once they had their country back. They would certainly never agree to cede any of their country to Iraq, especially the more profitable parts. Not least, Saddam would not risk the potential loss of face attending a unilateral withdrawal from Kuwait and repeal of its annexation. As a result, he never himself acted as if a diplomatic solution, based on a combination of withdrawal from Kuwait and a face-saver, was readily available. Failing to engage in an active search for an escape route, his response to the various formulas offered by anxious third parties and regional allies was generally dismissive. War, as Saddam gradually concluded, was infinitely better than unilateral withdrawal. Caught between the risks of unconditional withdrawal and the risks, but also the opportunities, of an armed confrontation, the choice seemed self-evident. Were he to succeed in holding on against the coalition for some time, war would offer Saddam the best chance for political survival and even a final victory. Just as the Egyptian President Gamal Abd Al-Nasser had managed to turn his country's military defeat in the 1956 Suez campaign, against a Franco-Anglo-Israeli coalition, into a resounding political victory, so Saddam seemingly hoped that the loss of Kuwait in a war with the allies would make him a hero, lauded by the Arab masses as a new Nasser, a leader who defied world imperialism and survived. To judge by his buoyant popularity among the Arab masses a decade later, this assessment seems to have been correct.

And here no doubt lies the foremost source of Saddam's danger and the war's greatest value. In a political system where absolute leaders supersede state institutions and the notion of national interest is highly personalized; where no orderly mechanisms for political participation and peaceful transfer of power exist; and where the goal of regime survivability supersedes everything else, physical force has become the foremost mode of political discourse. Should Saddam, or for that matter any other Middle Eastern dictator, deem himself to be in mortal danger, he would have no scruples about using all means at his disposal to protect himself: including chemical, biological or even nuclear weapons, whether against his own population or external enemies, real or imaginary.

Had Iraq not invaded Kuwait in the first place, it would have most probably become a nuclear power by the early 1990s. As things were, the Gulf War temporarily arrested Saddam's dogged quest for the bomb and laid the ground for the complete eradication of Iraq's nuclear infrastructure through the strictest arms control regime ever to have been imposed on a member of the international community. Fortunately for Saddam, Western leaders failed to grasp the centrality of these weapons in his Hobbesian world-view. To the Iraqi dictator, nuclear weapons have always meant much more than the 'great equalizer'. They have been a personal obsession: a symbol of Iraq's technological prowess, a prerequisite for regional hegemony, the ultimate guarantee of the survival of his personal rule. Hence, Saddam was determined to salvage whatever he could from his nuclear program, come what may, and for years played an intricate cat-and-mouse game with the UN Security Council over Iraq's non-conventional disarmament. Exploiting to the full the shortness of international memory, manifested *inter alia* in deep disputes in the anti-Iraq coalition about the maintenance of the sanctions, Saddam emerged victorious from his struggle with the UN, removing in the late 1990s the arms inspectors from Iraqi territory. This in turn meant that, within the foreseeable future, Iraq, as well as Iran, which for some time has been pursuing its own nuclear program, will have entered the nuclear club. The Middle East may thus become the first ever region to experience a nuclear war.

While the Gulf War failed to contain the Middle East's drift towards the nuclear age, it has nevertheless accelerated a number of regional developments, most notably the Arab–Israeli peace process. Reflecting the gradual disillusionment by both parties with the utility of armed force as a foreign policy instrument, this process can be traced to the 1967 Six Day War, which dealt militant pan-Arabism a mortal blow. It continued with the 1973 War, which shattered Israel's brief illusion of prowess created by the 1967 War. And while the impact of these wars sufficed to produce the Egyptian–Israeli peace treaty of 1979, another decade of intense violence was required to wear down the more intransigent players on both sides.

The eight-year war between Iraq and Iran drove home to many Arabs that Israel was not the principal threat to their national security. Similarly, the disastrous Lebanon War convinced many Israelis that there was no military solution to the Arab–Israeli conflict.[3] No less importantly, the war destroyed the military infrastructure of the PLO in Lebanon and sowed the seeds of the uprising in the occupied territories (*intifada*) which allowed the PLO to ostensibly shed its commitment to Israel's destruction and to accept the hitherto blasphemous formula of a two-state solution: Israel, and a Palestinian state in the territory of Mandatory Palestine. Even Saddam was not deterred from seeking Israeli weapons for his war against Iran, or from voicing public support for peace negotiations between the Arabs and Israel: 'No Arab leader looks forward to the destruction of Israel', he claimed, adding that any solution to the conflict must include 'the existence of a secure state for the Israelis'.[4]

The 1991 Gulf War reinforced and accelerated these developments by driving the final nail in the coffin of regional rejectionism. For the first time in their history, Israelis and Arabs found themselves in the same boat, as Saddam sought to legitimize his predatory move by portraying it as a noble attempt to promote the liberation of Palestine from Zionist occupation. While the falsehood of this linkage was eminently transparent, the widespread emotional eruption it caused, particularly when Saddam began firing his missiles at Israel, underscored the explosiveness of the Israeli–Palestinian conflict, if left unattended. No less importantly, Saddam's behavior constituted a painful reminder to the Arab regimes that Israel was not necessarily the main threat to their national security. This exceptional convergence of destinies led to tacit collaboration between Israel and the Arab members of the anti-Iraq coalition: the former kept the lowest possible profile, even refraining from retaliation after Iraq's missile attacks, while the latter highlighted the hollowness of Saddam's Palestinian pretensions and participated in the war operations against Iraq. This, in turn, would make it easier for the US administration to kick off the Madrid peace process shortly after the war.

Another spur towards Arab–Israeli reconciliation was given by the PLO's decision to side with Saddam Hussein. This folly cost it dearly. The Gulf monarchies were neither forgiving nor forgetful. As the primary financiers of the Palestinian cause, they felt betrayed by their beneficiaries; as hosts to a large population of Palestinian workers they felt threatened. This state of mind was illustrated not only by the harsh treatment of Palestinians in the newly liberated Kuwait and the political ostracizing of the PLO: within a month from the end of the war Saudi financial support for the PLO had been cut off, driving the organization to the verge of bankruptcy. Starved of financial resources, marginalized at the Madrid peace process, launched in October 1991, increasingly overpowered in the occupied territories by the Hamas militant Islamic movement, and beset by growing internal infighting, the PLO was desperate for political rehabilitation, and Yasir Arafat for a personal comeback. This was provided by the Oslo Accords of September 1993, which gave the PLO a new lease of life and put it, by the turn of the twenty-first century, in control of some 40 per cent of the territory and 99 per cent of the Palestinian population of the West Bank and the Gaza Strip.

However, at a crucial moment in the negotiations, during the July 2000 Camp David summit with Prime Minister Barak and President Clinton, Arafat declined the Israeli offer of over 90 per cent of the territories in return for peace, preferring instead to wage a lengthy war of attrition. This underscores his opportunistic perception of the Oslo Accords, and for that matter the tenacity of Arab refusal to accept the fact of Israel's existence. Begrudgingly forced into the negotiations process by the regional and international developments noted above, Arab leaders have shown to have had few qualms about reneging on this political course when the balance seemed to be tilting in their favor. Just as in 1991 Saddam fired dozens of missiles at Israel and vowed to eradicate the Jewish state in what seemed a total contradiction of his former rhetoric of peace overtures to Israel several years earlier, so the Palestinian leadership has repeatedly emphasized the tactical nature of its agreements with Israel, indicating the extent of Arab reluctance in general to acquiesce in the reality of a Jewish state.

The Gulf War might not have been powerful enough to change the general course of Arab–Israeli relations, but it has nevertheless underscored three interrelated historical trends that have long influenced Middle Eastern affairs. To start with, it has raised a serious question mark on the existence of a 'clash of civilizations' between the Middle East and the West.[5] As the Iraqi Foreign Minister, Tariq Aziz, told US Secretary of State James Baker during their meeting in Geneva on the eve of the Gulf War, the Americans were deluding themselves in believing that Iraq would confront Arab forces on the battlefield, since:

> the soldier in our region does not fight only when ordered to do so. Indeed he fights out of convictions ... Against the backdrop of your ties with Israel, I would like to tell you in all sincerity that if you initiate military action against an Arab country, you will be faced with hostile sentiment in the region, and in many Muslim states as well.[6]

That this confident prognosis failed to materialize provides further proof, if such is needed, that the gap between Middle Eastern and Western ruling classes is far narrower than is commonly assumed. Moreover, notwithstanding their differences, there have been striking resemblances in the historical development of the worlds of Islam and Christianity. Both harbored universal aspirations underpinned by unwavering feelings of superiority, and both used the vehicle of empire to make their bid, first for the control of the Mediterranean, then for global domination, converting *en masse* the vast populations coming under their sway by either peaceful or violent means. Indeed, the millenarian confrontation between the Middle East and the West, with its vicious circle of '*jihad* and Crusade, conquest and reconquest', has essentially been a struggle for imperial mastery rather than a 'clash of civilizations'.[7]

As their domain came under growing European pressure, Muslim and Middle Eastern rulers proved increasingly pragmatic, interested far more in the temporal goal of imperial preservation than in the practice of *jihad*. This in turn has led, since the early nineteenth century, to the advent of a symbiotic pattern of pragmatic cooperation and conflict. For all their vibrant religious, nationalistic and anti-colonialist rhetoric, Middle Eastern states and regimes have had few qualms about seeking the support and protection of the 'infidel' powers they have been vilifying – against fellow Arabs or Muslims – whenever their interests have so required. Just as the Ottoman Empire used the great European powers to ensure its own continued survival, so Egyptian President Nasser introduced large numbers of Soviet troops into Egypt when confronted with an unmanageable Israeli threat, and Khomeini, the personification of radical Islam, was not deterred from acquiring weapons from the 'Great Satan', the United States, in order to save the Islamic Republic.

This political cooperation has of course been purely instrumental and accompanied by no corresponding acceptance of Western doctrines and values, as its most notorious recent exponent, Saddam Hussein, has continually shown. Yet its scope and pervasiveness underscore the supremacy of pragmatic considerations over manichean ideals in contemporary Middle Eastern affairs.

Secondly, the Gulf War dealt a body blow to the popular perception of Middle Eastern history as an offshoot of global power politics by proving yet again that the main impetus for regional developments is provided by the local actors and that great-power influences, however potent, play a secondary role.[8] Thus, not only was the entire Gulf crisis triggered by Iraq's invasion of Kuwait, but the vast international coalition, headed by the United States, then at the height of its prowess as the 'only remaining superpower', failed to persuade Saddam to leave the emirate and was forced to go to war to achieve this goal. Moreover, even this war would not have been possible, had Saudi Arabia not allowed the use of its territory as a springboard for the anti-Iraq campaign. That it chose to do this, despite the extreme sensitivity of deploying 'infidel' forces on Islam's holiest lands, a fact exploited to the full by Saddam, was not due to American persuasiveness but rather to the fear of an Iraqi invasion. Furthermore, the impact of the American military victory gradually evaporated. The American hegemonic power began to be felt again only after its forceful intervention in Afghanistan.

Finally, the Gulf War exposed the hollowness of the notion of pan-Arabism. Since its formation in the wake of the First World War, the contemporary Middle Eastern nation-state system has been under sustained assault as an artificial creation of

Western imperialism at variance with local yearnings for regional unity. Intellectuals and politicians have repeatedly urged its destruction. National leaders – from Gamal Abd Al-Nasser, to Ayatollah Khomeini, to Saddam Hussein – have justified their constant interference in the affairs of other states by claiming to do precisely that.

And yet this system has proved to be extremely resilient, withstanding all challenges to its existence by Arab nationalists seeking to 'eliminate the traces of Western imperialism' and unify the so-called 'Arab nation'. This, in turn, proves that this far-from-perfect solution has been more in line with local realities than the vision of a unified regional order for the simple reason that there is not, and has never existed, an 'Arab nation' in the modern sense of the word: its invocation has been nothing but a clever ploy to rally popular support behind the quest for regional mastery. Before the 1920s and 1930s, when Arabs began to be indoctrinated with the notion that they all constituted one nation, there had been no general sense of 'Arabism' among the Arabic-speaking populations of the Middle East, only an intricate web of local loyalties to one's clan, tribe, village, town, religious sect or localized ethnic minority – overarched by submission to the Ottoman sultan-caliph in his capacity as the religious and temporal head of the world-wide Muslim community.

Had this disposition been allowed to run its natural course, these disparate communities would have developed into 'normal' nation-states and would have been spared the artificial schizophrenia instilled into them by imperialistically minded rulers and regimes. As things were, the systematic pan-Arab indoctrination sufficed to create a deep dissonance between the reality of state nationalism and the dream of an empire packaged as a unified 'Arab nation'. It failed, however, to make any headway towards the creation of such a nation. For even 'imagined communities' cannot be invented *deus ex machina* but must rather be grounded, however tenuously, in the real world.

It is precisely this insubstantial nature of 'Arab nationalism' that has turned the Arab–Israeli conflict into the main, indeed the only, common denominator of pan-Arab solidarity. For it is infinitely easier to foment collective hatred of the other than to create a genuine national solidarity among disparate populations with nothing in common apart from shared language and religion. Had the Arab masses not been systematically brainwashed for decades, most of them would have been totally oblivious to the existence of their Palestinian 'brothers', let alone the 'Zionist movement' and its alleged usurpation of 'Arab land'. In the event, pan-Arab indoctrination has managed to generate pervasive hatred of Jews and Israelis but not a real solidarity that could drive the Arab masses voluntarily to sacrifice their well-being on the altar of the Palestinian cause.

Still, by transforming the bilateral Israeli–Palestinian feud into a multilateral conflict, pan-Arabism has prolonged its duration, increased its intensity and made its resolution far more complex and tortuous. It has done so by rejecting both the Jewish right to national self-determination and Palestinian nationalism (or for that matter any other Arab state nationalism) and insisting on their incorporation into a wider Arab framework. No less important, it has instilled unrealistic visions, hopes and expectations in Palestinian political circles at key junctures. The consequence has been to deny Palestinians the right to determine their own fate.

By underscoring the supremacy of Arab state nationalism over the pan-Arab ideal, and by exposing the hollowness of Saddam's pan-Arab pretensions, the 1991 Gulf War has done the Middle East a great service. For it is only when the imperial pan-Arab dream no longer occupies a central place in the aspirations of the Middle East's political classes and is replaced by a general acceptance of the region's diversity that its inhabitants will move towards a new stability that transcends present-day norms.

NOTES

1. Mohamed Heikal, *Illusions of Triumph: An Arab View of the Gulf War* (London: Harper Collins, 1992), p. 200.
2. Efraim Karsh and Inari Rautsi, *Saddam Hussein: A Political Biography* (New York: Free Press, 1991) p. 2.
3. Efraim Inbar, 'Arab–Israeli Coexistence: The Causes, Achievements and Limitations', *Israel Affairs*, 6 (Spring/Summer 2000), pp. 258–61.

4. *International Herald Tribune*, 27 November, 5 December 1984.
5. Samuel Huntington, *The Clash of Civilizations* (New York: Simon & Schuster, 1996).
6. FBIS, NES, 92-009, 14 January 1992.
7. For such a view of Middle Eastern international politics, see Efraim Karsh and Inari Karsh, *Empires of Sand: The Struggle for Mastery in the Middle East, 1789–1923* (Cambridge, MA: Harvard University Press, 1999).
8. Efraim Karsh, 'Cold War, Post-Cold War: Does it Make a Difference in the Middle East?', in Efraim Inbar and Gabriel Sheffer (eds), *The National Security of Small States in a Changing World* (London: Frank Cass, 1997), pp. 77–106.

Index

Printed in the United Kingdom
by Lightning Source UK Ltd.
119576UK00001B/34-39

9 780714 683058